Data Processing Documentation and Procedures Manual

Data Processing Documentation and Procedures Manual

LARRY E. LONG
Lehigh University

RESTON PUBLISHING COMPANY, INC.
Reston, Virginia
A Prentice-Hall Company

Library of Congress Cataloging in Publication Data

Long, Larry E
Data processing documentation and procedures manual.

Includes index.
1. Electronic data processing documentation.
I. Title.
QA76.9.D167 658′.04 78-27101
ISBN 0-8359-1237-X

Reston Publishing Company, Inc.
A Prentice-Hall Company
Reston, Virginia 22090

10 9 8 7 6 5 4 3 2

Printed in the United States of America.

To Nancy

Contents

Part II
SYSTEM DEVELOPMENT AND IMPLEMENTATION

Part IV
HARDWARE AND SOFTWARE EVALUATION AND SELECTION

Preface

From their inception, computer centers follow very similar growth patterns and suffer many of the same growing pains. Virtually every computer center has experienced, or will experience, the consequences of the lack of standardized documentation and procedures. The Data Processing Documentation and Procedures Manual (called "DP Manual" for short) is designed for use by a computer center whose management and personnel have recognized the importance of systems and general computer center documentation and of internal and external DP procedures standardization. The DP Manual is intended to minimize the effort required to develop a standardized documentation and procedures package while maximizing the effectiveness and usefulness of the final product.

Though few corporate officers will admit it, the computer center is becoming, or perhaps already is, the nucleus of corporate operations. As the scope and integration of computer-based information systems increases, so will the corporate dependency on the computer center for a smooth and efficient operation. Unfortunately, because of the inordinate corporate demands, personnel turnover, and lack of standardized DP procedures, computer centers as a whole are not well organized (often through no fault of DP management). Implementation of the DP Manual will help curb inordinate corporate demands by standardizing DP procedures and will ease the pain of the loss of key personnel through the judicious use of documentation.

There exists a myriad of approaches to the development of a DP Manual—this manual illustrates one approach and its final product. The DP Manual is based on a standardized system development methodology, which is presented, in depth, in the manual. The approach used emphasizes two very important aspects of successful computer center operation. First, the user and top management are continually involved as a matter of policy and according to standard procedures. Second, in order to eliminate misunderstandings and numerous subsequent revisions of previous work, all communications and documentation are written according to a comprehensive set of instructions. The manual is not limited to documentation and procedures for systems and programming; it also encompasses all aspects of routine computer center operation.

The approach taken in the preparation of this manual was to make it as ready-to-use as possible. It is 90 to 100 percent ready-to-use depending upon what minor local changes would be required. Many computer centers cannot afford the luxury of dedicating 1 to 3 man-years of effort to the development of a DP documentation and procedures manual (especially when there is no guarantee that the end result will be acceptable). This manual will enable computer center staff to implement a comprehensive set of standardized documentation practices and procedures with a minimum expenditure of time and effort. Implementing the complete DP Manual is not necessary. Using specific forms and/or procedures, or even parts of each, may be helpful.

The implementation of the DP Documentation and Procedures Manual can have a very positive effect on management efficiency. The DP Manual provides an excellent vehicle for project management. It includes project management aids made possible by the standardized methodology and project management procedures. The aids enable management to gather historical data that will aid in future project resource estimation. The basic project management procedures set forth in the DP Manual can be easily automated on an in-house basis. The DP Manual eases the requirement for DP management to direct every activity by detailing each person's responsibilities and tasks. The procedures detailed in the DP Manual dictate that DP efforts be channelled to projects on a priority basis and only when resources become available. As a result of establishing rigorous project initiation procedures, management will probably experience substantial decreases (up to 75 percent) in the number of work requests.

The DP Manual is divided into four parts. Part I, System Documentation and Procedures in the DP Environment, discusses documentation in general and explains how to use the remainder of the manual. Part II, System Development and Implementation, provides a vehicle by which comprehensive system and program documentation can be routinely compiled and maintained for on-line and batch systems, and a set of standard procedures for system development that are intended to improve the programmer–analyst–management interface and the DP–user interface. These procedures should substantially increase the effectiveness of all persons concerned in system development and implementation. Part III, General Computer Center Documentation, contains techniques for documenting computer center hardware, defining the organizational structure and personnel functions, and establishing a comprehensive training and career development program. Finally, Part IV, Hardware and Software Evaluation and Selection, presents a standard procedure, complete with forms and instructions, for the evaluation and selection of computer hardware and software. Parts III and IV address areas of computer center documentation and procedures that traditionally have been overlooked in favor of the crisis-oriented system development process; however, the importance of these areas is becoming more visible as computer centers become operationally more complex.

Part II, System Development and Implementation, because of its unique format, needs further explanation. The format of Part II is unique within the industry. All user–DP activities and documentation forms are conveniently interrelated via work flow diagrams. This completely integrated approach to systems development provides a master plan by which both users and DP professionals can be proactive, rather than reactive, to each other during system development and implementation. Part II, which is hardware and software independent, contains three types of documentation—intermediate, permanent, and project management. The intermediate documentation is a vehicle by which analysts and programmers can make orderly transitions through the various phases of the system development process. Permanent documentation provides for a comprehensive description of all facets of a given information system. Project management documentation provides the framework for scheduling, control, and evaluation of projects.

Every entry in every form of Part II was carefully studied with respect to usefulness, maintainability, space requirements, responsibility, and redundancy. These entries were screened so that only those that are absolutely necessary are included in the permanent documentation. Where possible, forms are designed in a matrix format, which is easy to complete and use. Those pieces of documentation that are primarily text are completed on a more flexible general purpose form. Each form has instructions that include purpose, assignment of responsibility, and specific instructions for the completion of each entry. Design and maintenance of data base management systems have been incorporated into the procedures and forms of the DP Manual.

Part III, Chapter 8, "Hardware Documentation: Computer, Peripherals, Communications," details a standardized procedure and a methodology for maintaining an up-to-date Hardware Configuration Chart complete with the hardware specifications necessary for hardware selection and interfacing, and for systems analysis and design. Chapter 9, "Structural Organization and Personnel," formally establishes the lines of authority, responsibilities, and duties of all computer center personnel. For the purposes of morale, personnel retention, and maintaining state-of-the-art expertise, each computer center should maintain a training and career development program. Chapter 10, "Training and Career Development," provides an effective and efficient method for establishing and maintaining such a program.

The decision to purchase or lease a particular proprietary software package, a new computer system, or a computer service could have far reaching effects on the corporation. Therefore, these decisions should be based on the best available information and a rigorous evaluation and selection methodology. Part IV presents an evaluation and selection methodology that ensures that all facets of the decision process are investigated and properly evaluated.

The DP Manual should prove useful to all persons involved in DP management: systems analysts, programmers, data base administrators, users of DP, and people in specialized positions dealing with DP standards, documentation, and procedures. A given computer center could save several man-years of effort by adopting the DP Manual in its entirety. However, if the manual as a whole is not appropriate, each of the above named persons can extract hundreds of ideas, approaches, methods, and/or procedures from the DP Manual. Used in this manner, the DP Manual can still save man-months, perhaps even man-years, of effort.

The DP Manual was written as a professional DP reference manual; however, it is an excellent supplemental text for college/university courses in systems analysis and design. Most texts in this area are usually too general and lack the detail necessary to give the student a good feel for the systems development process. The DP Manual contains a concise, yet complete methodology, which explicitly defines the job functions of the various DP professionals and implicitly defines the "real world" in which the DP professional works. Also, any class projects, systems analysis, and/or programming can be completed utilizing the procedures set forth in the DP Manual. The DP Manual has been tried, and proven effective, in the university classroom.

The successful computer centers of today and tomorrow have or will have DP documentation and procedures manuals of some kind. The need for DP project management, the mobility of DP personnel, the increasing requests from auditors to investigate certain aspects of computer-based information systems, and the complexity of on-line systems development are among the factors that make an internal DP manual an absolute necessity. This DP Manual will be of help in the improvement and/or preparation of such manuals.

Larry E. Long

I

System Documentation and Procedures in the DP Environment

1

Documentation Principles and Practices

System and System Development Documentation

Perhaps the single most important ingredient for the ultimate success in an automated data processing environment is strict adherence to sound documentation principles and practices by both user and DP personnel both during system development and after implementation. Certainly construction of an office building would not begin until plans had been drawn and approved by all concerned. And so it is with developing a new computer system. System documentation provides the foundation for the development of the computer system and provides a mechanism to ensure that the system will accomplish the original objectives. After system implementation there is a need to maintain a computer system just as there is a need to perform maintenance on a skyscraper. For efficient maintenance, system documentation is as necessary for a computer system as a blueprint is for a building.

Documentation is often thought of as noncreative by both user and DP personnel alike. It is, and has been in the past (in less sophisticated DP environments), given a very low priority during and after the system development process. Therefore, any documentation compiled at project completion was usually haphazard and incomplete (sometimes causing more harm than good).

In DP, there is always another fire to fight, and too often the emphasis has been on implementation at any cost. System documentation has been brushed over lightly, if at all, and another fire fight begins. An unsuccessful DP shop can operate indefinitely without establishing formal standards for documentation. The Data Processing Documentation and Procedures Manual (the DP Manual) provides a mechanism for insuring that standard procedures, as well as proper documentation principles and practices, are adhered to during the system development process and after system implementation (Part II).

Documentation takes personnel time, and consequently added costs are incurred. However, it should be noted, and often it is not, that the savings in personnel time as a result of proper documentation far exceed the costs over the long run. The following reasons highlight the cost effectiveness of system documentation. System documentation:

1. Provides a vehicle for review of the system. Standard review plateaus during the system development process are made easy by the timely presentation of accumulated system documentation. The project should be continuously reviewed to ensure an efficient and effective result. Many times a subpar system is implemented because review procedures are nonexistent.
2. Provides a mechanism for monitoring project progress and evaluating personnel effectiveness by standardizing the procedures of the system development process. The DP Manual contains Work Flow Diagrams that graphically depict these procedures, making possible the use of Work Progress Charts.
3. Minimizes problems with personnel absenteeism and turnover. DP Managers today cannot afford to be dependent upon individuals for certain segments or all of a system. The computer center should be capable of operating independently of any group or individual. Standards and documentation can help make any computer system people-independent. The people-independence aspect provides a greater flexibility to expose systems analysts and programmers to a variety of systems rather than strapping them to "their baby."
4. Provides material by which operational people can be trained to use the system. A verbal description is always less satisfactory than a well-written description of the system operation. This documentation can aid in the development of training programs and be used for day-to-day references by users and DP personnel.
5. Provides a mechanism for maintenance of the system. Any modifications or updates to the system procedures and/or programs may require three or four times the manpower without the proper documentation as a guideline, and may require even more manpower if the person who developed the program is no longer available.

The system development documentation of Part II in the DP Manual can be classified, for discussion purposes, into five categories:

1. *Feasibility Study Documentation.* This documentation includes the documents that are prepared for the purpose of evaluating the feasibility of a proposed system or system upgrade. Also included in this set of documentation are those documents that present an overall but general description of both the proposed and present systems. The feasibility study advocated in this manual is comprehensive in

nature and eliminates the requirement for a general system design.

2. *System Documentation.* This documentation, as compiled by the systems analysts, is a description of the user's DP requirements, and is a complete and thorough picture of the system. This documentation should be all that the programmer needs to complete the required programming.
3. *Program Documentation.* This documentation is prepared by the programmers in order to aid in program development and to document the programs once they have been completed.
4. *Operations Documentation.* This documentation is prepared by either or both the systems analysts and programmers. It serves to define the operational functions, relative to a particular system, of data entry personnel, operators, librarians, control clerks in DP, and other functional personnel in user departments.
5. *Project Control.* This set of documentation comprises all records that are peripheral to the definition of the actual system and comprises progress, cost, budget, manpower, and machine time reports. Project control documentation is required throughout the system development process.

The documentation from the feasibility study should serve as the framework for a comprehensive system design, but will become obsolete as detail documentation becomes available. The documentation required by the standard procedures of this manual may require many changes during the system development process and should be updated as required. Certain documents may serve only intermediate purposes and become inappropriate at certain stages during the system development process. However, after implementation of the system, certain previously prepared standardized documents (latest update) will serve as permanent documentation for use in system maintenance and operation. The former is called intermediate documentation, and the latter is called permanent documentation.

It should be noted that all systems should not be documented with the same rigor and depth. A new financial information system which will be used every day for years should be carefully documented; on the other hand, a system developed to be run only once requires a minimum amount of documentation.

General Computer Center Documentation

The other documentation area presented in this manual relates generally to the computer center. The center should be documented with respect to hardware and personnel. Part III addresses this area of documentation.

1. *Hardware Documentation.* Hardware documentation, which usually does not relate to a particular system, is simply an up-to-date graphical summary of the relationships among the computer(s), peripherals, and communications equipment in the computer center(s) and their associated specifications. This summary aids both in system design and in any future equipment selections.
2. *Structural Organization and Personnel Documentation.* This documentation is a graphical display of the formal organization and committees of the computer center that illustrates lines of authority. Written position descriptions and committee charges are also included.
3. *Training and Career Development.* In order to formally establish career paths and a vehicle for personnel to advance within the ranks, a comprehensive training and career development plan should be documented and maintained for each DP employee in the company.

Hardware and Software Evaluation and Selection

Part IV, Hardware and Software Evaluation and Selection, presents a standardized methodology for hardware and software evaluation and selection. This process is presented as a set of standardized procedures using intermediate documentation to solicit comprehensive vendor responses that are in a standard format, thereby making the decision process more straightforward.

2

Use of the DP Documentation and Procedures Manual in System Development and Implementation

Introduction

Part II of the DP Manual, System Development and Implementation, is compiled as a professional reference manual and guide and, therefore, is not meant to be read in sequential order. Instead, the manual user will select the appropriate sections as the project progresses. The primary purpose of Part II is twofold. First, Part II provides a mechanism that, when used properly, can create a well-ordered DP environment during the system development process, resulting in a complete system documentation package at the conclusion of the project. Second, Part II of the DP Manual provides a structural approach to system development, which provides a timely review of project progress by appropriate groups and individuals (users, steering committee, and DP management). This approach is designed to eliminate, or at least minimize, the communication problems encountered during the system development process. The ultimate objective of Part II is to keep all involved persons informed via proper standardized documentation and progress checkpoints (review meetings).

Only Part II of the DP Manual requires special instructions for the user of the manual. Since Part III, General Computer Center Documentation, and Part IV, Hardware and Software Evaluation and Selection, require no special instructions, this chapter is devoted to Part II, System Development and Implementation.

Overview of Part II

The system development process is presented in three distinct phases.

Phase I—System Initiation and Feasibility Study

> *Note:* The feasibility study advocated in this DP Manual is comprehensive. Since the vast majority of duly commissioned feasibility studies are

ultimately accepted for implementation, the ultimate product of a feasibility study should be more than a simple yes or no. The feasibility study should accurately reflect the expected costs and enumerate the benefits, both tangible and intangible. The only reasonable approach to cost/benefit analysis is, essentially, to do the general system design, thereby defining the scope of the project. Almost every veteran DP professional has at one time experienced a substantial project cost and manpower overrun because the feasibility study was based on an abstract idea and not a design. Because of the comprehensive nature of the feasibility study, the documentation necessary to begin the detail system design is available at the conclusion of the feasibility study. Not only has the need for a general system design been eliminated, but everyone, users and DP personnel, understands what is to be done.

Phase II—System Analysis, Design, Programming, Conversion, and Implementation (subdivided into three parts)

Part 1—System Analysis and Design
Part 2—Programming
Part 3—Conversion and Implementation

Phase III—Evaluation and Ongoing Operation

Each of the three phases (and parts in Phase II) is presented separately in three sections (Work Flow Diagrams, Block Descriptions, and document and/or report forms with instructions). The following brief descriptions are followed by detailed explanations of each of the three sections.

Work Flow Diagrams. The entire system development process is depicted by using flowcharting techniques to illustrate the sequence and relationship of the various activities (216 in all). The Work Flow Diagrams provide the link for the three sections.

Block Descriptions. The activity for each required block in the Work Flow Diagrams is described in detail. The blocks are numbered by phase for ease of reference.

Document and/or Report Forms with Instructions. During the system development process, certain individuals or groups are required to document their decision, findings, and/or work. The required document forms and instructions are included in this section. It should be noted that certain forms may be classified as documents and others as reports. In order to eliminate confusion, any further reference to documents or reports will collectively reference the entire set of standardized instructions and forms. The two words are used interchangeably throughout the DP Manual.

Work Flow Diagrams

The Work Flow Diagrams are designed to include all major activities of individuals or groups involved in the system development process and to illustrate the sequence and relationship of these various activities. Use the Phase I Work Flow Diagram, page 20, as an illustrative aid while reading the following explanatory paragraphs.

Since the Work Flow Diagrams are referenced by many individuals with varying levels of flowchart understanding, a minimum set of flowchart symbols are used. The two main symbols used are the process and decision symbols. Note that no input/output (I/O) symbols are used. For the purpose of clarity and for simplification of the Work Flow Diagrams, I/O is noted in two ways. A specific output for a decision or process is noted by a reference to a document number at the lower righthand corner of the block. The output accumulates throughout the process, and any or all of the output package becomes input to any decision or process block. The documentation package is available and up to date at any time during the process; therefore, the input is implied. Specific input requirements for any process or decision are so noted in the Block Descriptions.

The other flowchart symbols used in the Work Flow Diagrams are connectors (on-page and off-page) and terminal symbols, which are self-explanatory.

Each symbol referred to as *block* in the Work Flow Diagrams (except connectors and terminal symbols) is numbered, starting with 1 for each phase. This number can be found outside the upper left corner of the block. Note that these numbers do not necessarily depict the order of execution of the activities. Their purpose is to serve as a cross-reference mechanism to the Block Description that elaborates on the activity defined in that particular block.

Just outside the lower right corner of certain blocks, a document number can be found. The document or report number (a Roman numeral I, II, or III, which indicates phase, followed by a two- or three-digit number) indicates the specific document or report output for the activity depicted by that block.

Block Descriptions

A Block Description is given for each process and decision and for some terminal symbols in the Work Flow Diagrams. It is not physically possible to fully describe most activities within the space allocated. Therefore, a brief descriptive phrase is presented in each block and a reference (block number) is made to a Block Description, which contains a complete word picture of the activities within that block. Refer to the Phase I Block Descriptions on page 22 for example Block Descriptions.

The type of information included in a Block Description could be personnel involved, responsibilities, specifics for report preparation (if not included in report instructions), criteria for decisions, approaches to a solution, information (previous reports) required for a decision, etc.

After DP personnel and users become familiar with the process, the brief descriptive phrases in the Work Flow Diagrams should suffice. For these people the Block Descriptions will serve as backup and reference materials, but for most users and new DP personnel they will continue to be essential.

The block format is used merely to provide a standard framework for project development tasks. It is not intended to impede creativity and personal initiative.

Document and/or Report Forms with Instructions

The instructions for report preparation and the specific forms used for report preparation are included in this section. The report instructions are presented and are followed by the specific form to be used in generating that report. However, note that not all report instructions are followed by a form. In these cases a general purpose form or the form of another report is utilized. This is so noted on the report instructions. Refer to Phase I report forms and instructions, starting on page 33, while reading the following explanatory paragraphs.

The reports required during the system development process and ultimately for system documentation are numbered by association with the phase in which they are first used. All reports initially used in Phase I are prefaced by a Roman numeral I, in Phase II by a II, and in Phase III by a III. The reports are numbered in each phase, by numbers 10 to 299 for Phase I; 300 to 499 for Phase II, Part I; 500 to 699 for Phase II, Part 2; 700 to 899 for Phase II, Part 3; and 900 to 999 for Phase III. For example, the Applications Description report number is I10. The report numbers are simply for reference purposes and are not numbered in sequence of use. Note that a Phase I report might also be used in Phase II (e.g., System Status Report, I140).

The instructions for any given report might reference a form with a number that starts with G. These are general purpose forms, which are used for a number of reports and documents. These forms are never referenced in the Work Flow Diagrams. They are only referenced in the instructions for specific reports. These general forms and instructions are contained in Part II, Chapter 7.

Note that all reports, whether reviewed or not, should be continually updated to reflect the current status of the system development project, and that not all findings, work, decisions, etc., are written up in a formal report or document. On many occasions the Feasibility Study Team Head (FSTH) or the Project Team Head (PTH) is required to write up an informal memo or report for internal use only. Certain types of information may be required for preparation of a formal report but may be of little value in the total system documentation package.

Maintenance of DP Manual and System Documentation

The responsibility for maintaining the DP Manual and maintaining all system documentation, based on standards set forth in the DP Manual, is that of the Systems Coordinator (SC). Depending upon the size of the computer center, the SC may wish to delegate authority for this function to a systems analyst; however, the responsibility still resides with the SC. He or she is responsible for the initial distribution and subsequent updates to the manual. Each department and/or division manager should have a copy of the DP Manual. Any revisions made to the DP Manual go through the SC, who in turn distributes the revisions and update instructions to holders of the manual. The SC is also responsible for maintenance of all system documentation after system implementation. For any given system the documentation is compiled as described in Phase II. The SC should maintain the master of the system documentation and a copy, which should be stored in a safe place. These are usually the only two copies of the total system documentation (computer center staff size may dictate a need for more than two).

Standardized Position Definitions

In order to standardize the system development process, certain positions need to be defined. Virtually every computer center manning document has these, or very similar, functional positions, even though the titles may vary from center to center. Prior to using this manual for systems development, the director of the computer center should designate persons to fill the Data Processing Manager, Systems Coordinator, and Operations Manager positions of this DP Manual.

Data Processing Manager (DPM). This individual is the primary interface between the users and the computer center and has line control within the computer center. In most cases, this position would be occupied by the director of the computer center; however, in medium-large and large centers the assistant manager may be designated as the DPM.

Systems Coordinator (SC). The systems coordinator is the nucleus of the standard procedures set forth in the DP Manual. In most computer centers this individual would occupy the position of systems manager or systems/programming manager.

Operations Manager (OM). In most computer centers the operations manager would control the machine room operations, data reduction, and control functions. In large centers the assistant manager of operations may be more appropriate than the actual operations manager for these tasks.

Two other positions noted in the DP Manual are standard throughout the industry.

Programmer. The programmers can be individuals who are titled programmer or programmer/analyst where duties are primarily programming in nature.

Systems Analyst (SA). The systems analysts can be individuals who are titled systems analysts or programmer/analysts where duties are primarily systems analysis.

Two other positions external to the computer center should be noted. These reference the user segment of the organization.

User. *User* collectively refers to persons involved in the development and/or operation of a computer-based information system and are not employed within the computer center.

User Head (UH). The term *user head* refers collectively to the head(s) (or manager(s)) of a division, department, and/or agency involved in the development and operation of a given system.

Several other positions are defined in the Block Descriptions and are filled temporarily by appointment. They are:

ISPC Head (ISPCH)—Phase I.

ISPC Liaison—Phase I.

Feasibility Study Team Head (FSTH)—Phase I.

Project Team Head (PTH)—Phase II, Part 1.

Lead Programmer (LP)—Phase II, Part 2.

Review Coordinator (RC)—Phase III.

The Information Systems Policy Committee

Responsibilities

Many companies do not have high-level DP steering committees such as the Information Systems Policy Committee (ISPC), or if they do, their charge is not sufficiently defined. If either of these situations reflects the current status of the existing steering committee, it is highly recommended that a high-level steering committee be established and/or formalized since the ISPC is an integral part of the computer center function. The responsibilities of the ISPC include:

1. Approving or rejecting requests for major DP services
2. Setting priorities among approved projects
3. Monitoring the progress of DP projects and the performance of ongoing systems using the procedures set forth in the DP Manual
4. Arbitrating differences between departments and/or divisions arising from DP operations
5. Setting policy that relates to DP and affects all departments
6. Developing short- and long-range plans for DP growth

Membership

The membership of the ISPC can take on a variety of formats. This paragraph contains, without any justification, one possible format. The ISPC might consist of a Vice-Presidential level person as Chairman (ISPC Head or ISPCH), 7 other voting members who have 2-year appointments, and the DPM as a permanent voting member. The ISPC has the responsibility of appointing 7 members who are selected from high-level user management. The appointments are subject to consent of both the individual concerned and his immediate manager. The ISPC is limited in voting members only; any person in high-level management may request a nonvoting seat on the committee and maintain it indefinitely. However, the total of voting and nonvoting members should not exceed 16.

Procedures

The ISPC functions to fulfill the responsibilities listed above. Responsibilities numbered 1, 2, and 3 involve ISPC participation in the system development process. The ISPC interface with this process is detailed in the DP Manual.

Only a voting member or his/her designated representative may cast a vote. The ISPCH votes only in the case of a tie. No vote will be taken when less than 6 voting members, or their representatives, are present.

A voting member must maintain a cumulative attendance record of at least 75%. Together, the member and his/her designated representative must maintain a cumulative attendance record of at least 90%. the ISPCH should act to appoint another ISPC member if a member becomes delinquent in either of the attendance categories.

The ISPC should meet at the discretion of the ISPCH. The Data Processing Manager or a user head should assist in scheduling meetings by communicating the need for a meeting directly to the ISPCH.

Standardized Forms

A complete set of forms for standardized systems development and documentation is contained in the DP Manual. The forms are obviously not to the appropriate scale, nor do they reflect the corporate logo, which certainly adds a touch of class but is not necessary. The forms, regular $8\frac{1}{2} \times 11$ inch and 11×16 inch size paper, fit neatly in standard three-ring binders. The larger forms are noted, below the illustration, as being 11×16 inches.

A company draftsman can reproduce the forms from the illustrations in the DP Manual (minus the circled references to the instructions), add the corporate logo, and/or make any revisions.

3

Condensed Work Flow Diagram of the System Development Process

The following page contains a Work Flow Diagram which is a condensed version of the more detailed Work Flow Diagrams contained in System Development and Implementation, Part II of the DP Manual. The purpose of the condensed version is to enable a DP Manual user to get an overview of the system development and implementation process without having to refer to the detailed Work Flow Diagrams. The condensed version depicts the process by phases. Note that in order to maintain consistency with the DP Manual, Phase II is shown in its three parts. The numbers by the upper left corner of each box indicate the blocks of the detailed Work Flow Diagrams that are condensed into that particular block. Should a user require any further detail, the user should refer to the detailed Work Flow Diagrams and the appropriate Block Descriptions in the System Development and Implementation section of the DP Manual.

Condensed Work Flow Diagrams

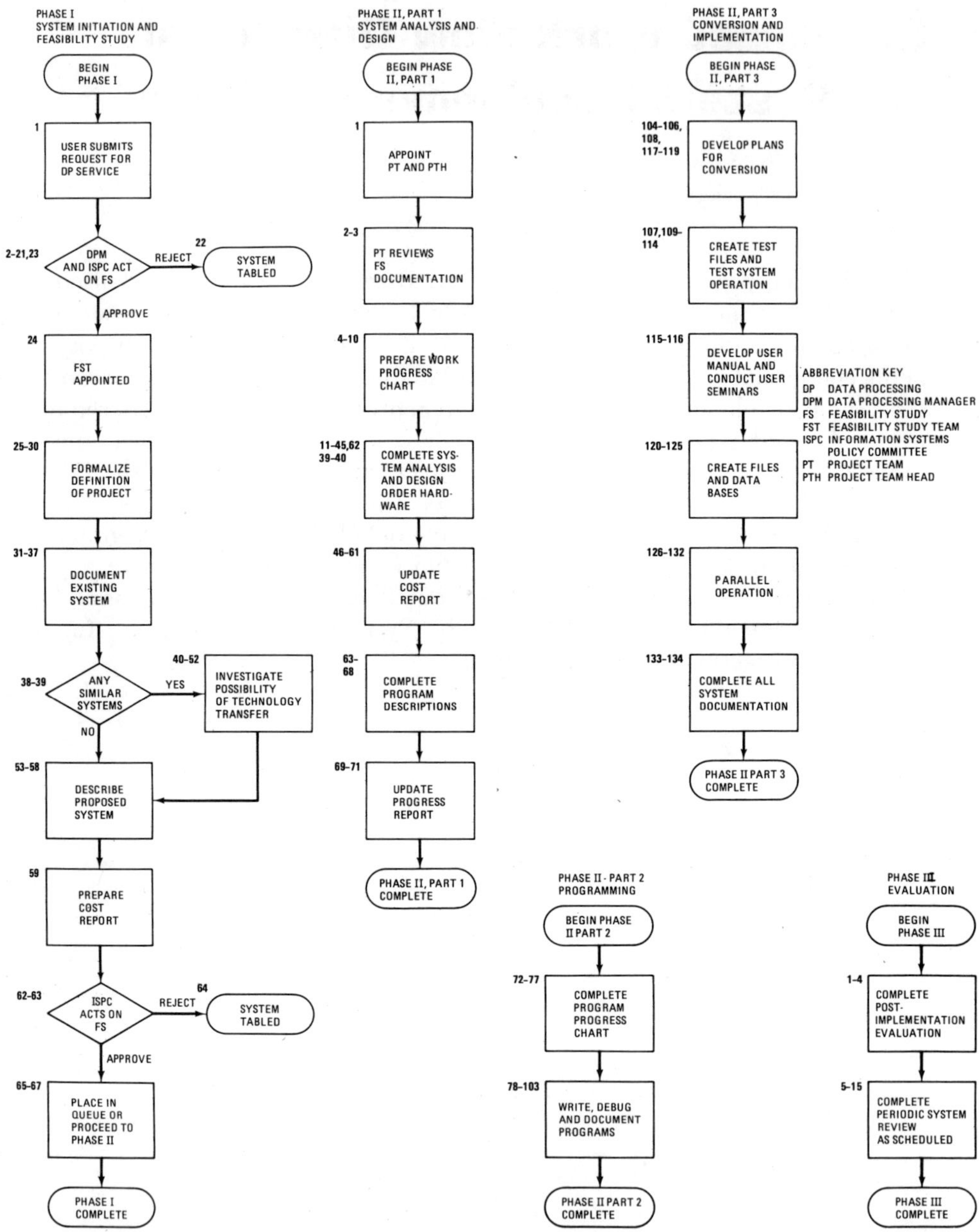

II

System Development and Implementation

4

Phase I—System Initiation and Feasibility Study

Work Flow Diagrams—Phase 1

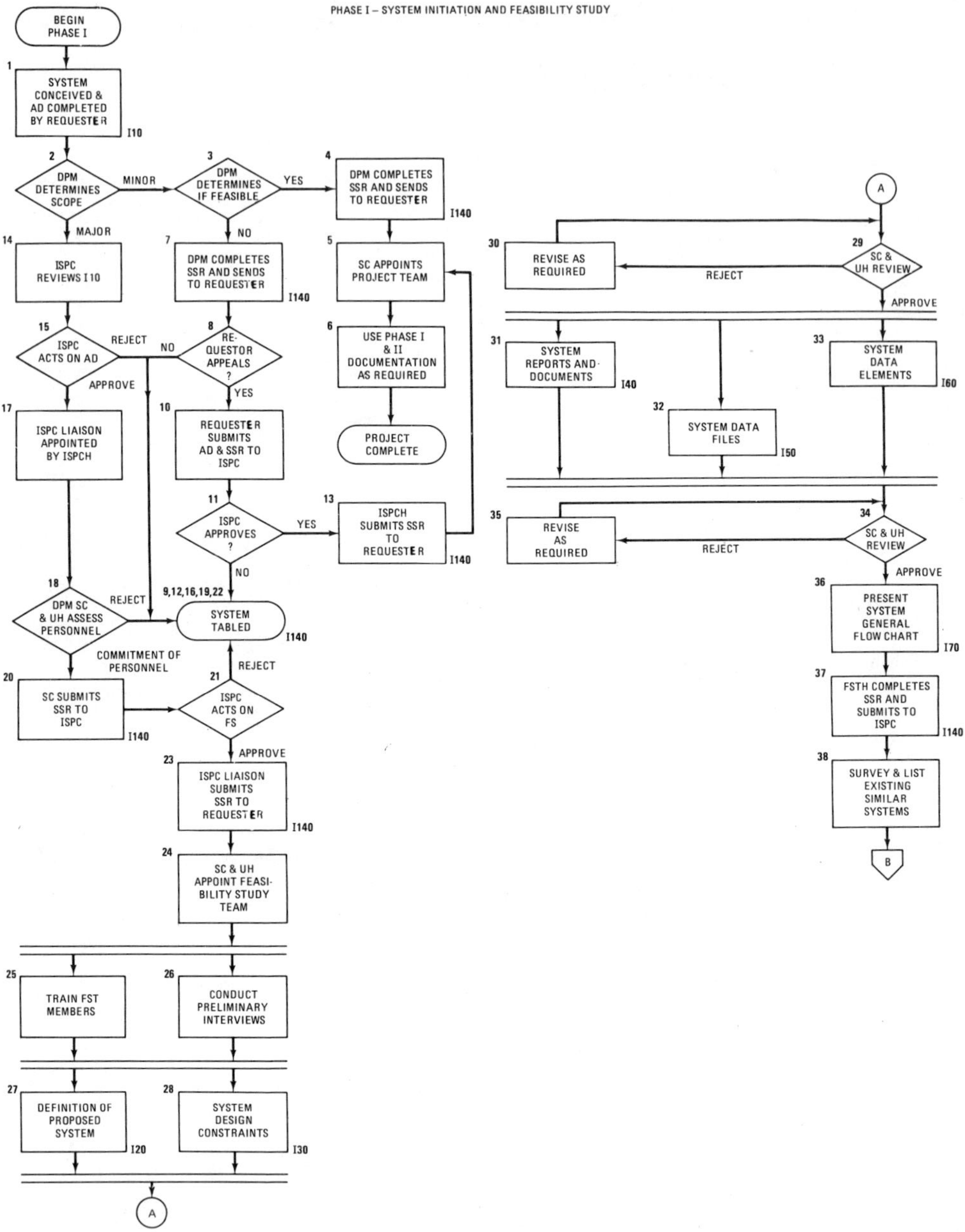

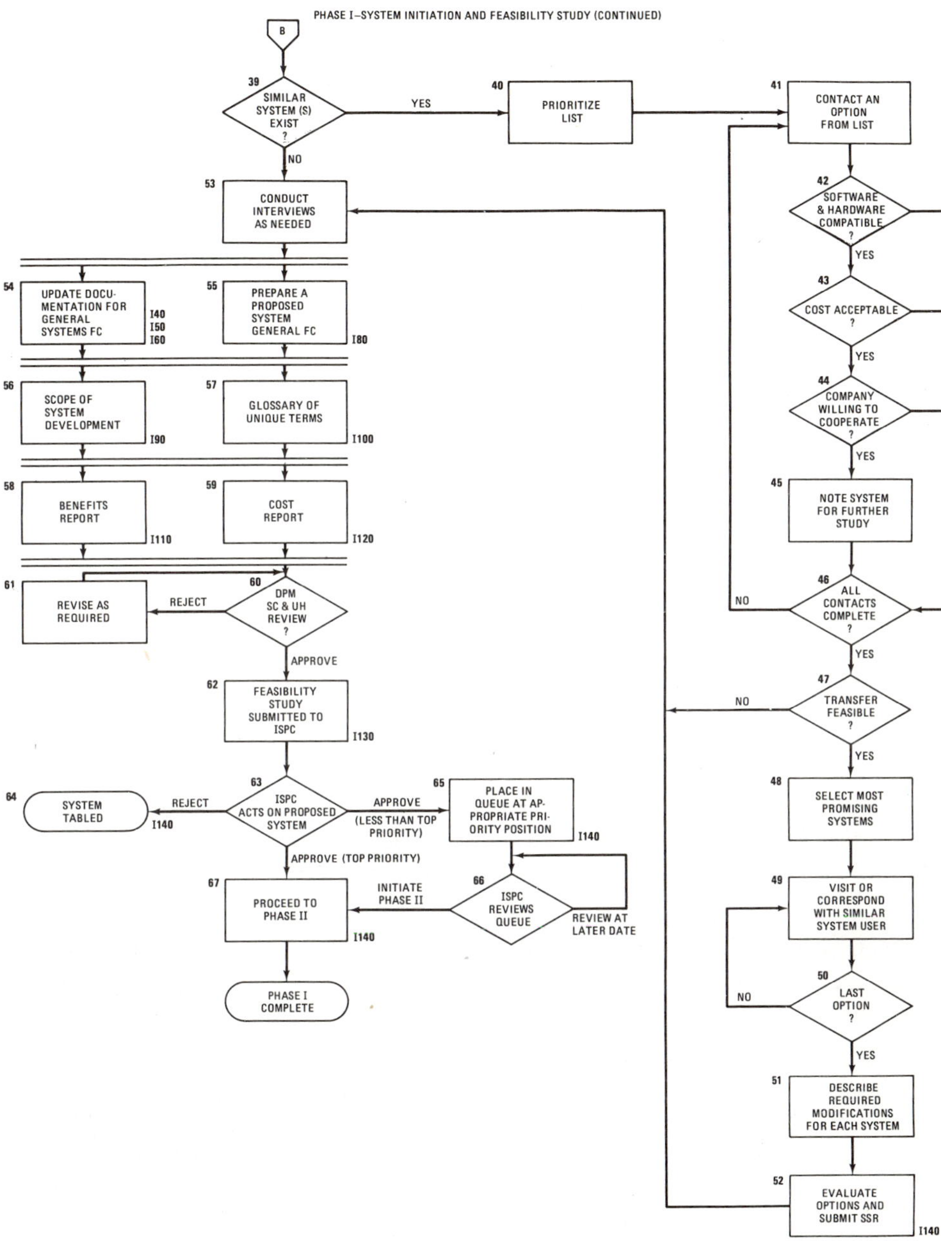
PHASE I–SYSTEM INITIATION AND FEASIBILITY STUDY (CONTINUED)
B
39 SIMILAR SYSTEM (S) EXIST ?
YES
NO
40 PRIORITIZE LIST
41 CONTACT AN OPTION FROM LIST
42 SOFTWARE & HARDWARE COMPATIBLE ?
43 COST ACCEPTABLE ?
44 COMPANY WILLING TO COOPERATE ?
45 NOTE SYSTEM FOR FURTHER STUDY
46 ALL CONTACTS COMPLETE ?
47 TRANSFER FEASIBLE ?
48 SELECT MOST PROMISING SYSTEMS
49 VISIT OR CORRESPOND WITH SIMILAR SYSTEM USER
50 LAST OPTION ?
51 DESCRIBE REQUIRED MODIFICATIONS FOR EACH SYSTEM
52 EVALUATE OPTIONS AND SUBMIT SSR
I140
53 CONDUCT INTERVIEWS AS NEEDED
54 UPDATE DOCU-MENTATION FOR GENERAL SYSTEMS FC
I40
I50
I60
55 PREPARE A PROPOSED SYSTEM GENERAL FC
I80
56 SCOPE OF SYSTEM DEVELOPMENT
I90
57 GLOSSARY OF UNIQUE TERMS
I100
58 BENEFITS REPORT
I110
59 COST REPORT
I120
60 DPM SC & UH REVIEW ?
REJECT
61 REVISE AS REQUIRED
APPROVE
62 FEASIBILITY STUDY SUBMITTED TO ISPC
I130
63 ISPC ACTS ON PROPOSED SYSTEM
REJECT
64 SYSTEM TABLED
I140
APPROVE (LESS THAN TOP PRIORITY)
65 PLACE IN QUEUE AT AP-PROPRIATE PRI-ORITY POSITION
I140
APPROVE (TOP PRIORITY)
66 ISPC REVIEWS QUEUE
REVIEW AT LATER DATE
INITIATE PHASE II
67 PROCEED TO PHASE II
I140
PHASE I COMPLETE

Block Descriptions—Phase 1

1. A suggestion for a new or improved computer applications system or subsystem could be initiated for several reasons and by several groups. A user or potential user may wish to automate an existing system, implement a system being used at another company, or purchase a commercial package. It is possible that corporate management might direct that a certain facet of the company be automated or upgraded. The Computer Center (CC) might suggest that a system be automated in order to augment or complement an existing system. The suggesting party is referred to as the requester.

The requester (with aid from a Computer Center systems analyst, if required) is responsible for completion of the Applications Description (AD), Form I10, which includes the proposed system's title, brief system description, background, time frame, funding source, etc. The completed AD is submitted to the Data Processing Manager (DPM) for review.

2. The DPM determines whether the development and implementation of the proposed system would require less than 3 professional (systems analysts and programmers) man-weeks of CC personnel time. If the DPM determines that the project will ultimately require more than 3 man-weeks, the AD, I10, is then sent to the Information Systems Policy Committee (ISPC) for review.

> *Note:* The 3 man-weeks is arbitrary. This figure could vary from 3 to 12 man-weeks depending upon the size of the computer center.

3. The DPM surveys available manpower, machine time, data resources, and other applicable constraints and limitations to determine if the proposed system is feasible and justified as described by the AD, I10. An examination of critical factors may require that the DPM enlist the aid of the Systems Coordinator (SC) and/or the Operations Manager (OM).

4. The DPM completes the System Status Report (SSR), Form I140, which reflects the acceptance of the proposed system as described in the Applications Description, and an estimated completion date. The SSR is sent to the requester.

5. Upon receiving notification of an approved proposed system, the Systems Coordinator then assigns systems analysts and/or programmers to the project as required. The SC then appoints a Project Team Head (PTH). The PTH should be a systems analyst if both a systems analyst and a programmer are required for project completion.

6. Since the scope of the project is small, the Phase II Work Flow Diagrams and documentation are used at the discretion of the PTH. The SC

should be kept informed of progress and should schedule review sessions with the users and DPM as, or if, required.

7. The DPM completes a System Status Report (SSR), I140, which reflects the disapproval of the proposed system and the SSR is sent to the requester. Appropriate comments should be included that relate the reasons for disapproving the proposed system.

8. The requester has the option of appealing the DPM's decision.

9. The proposed system is tabled. The AD, I10, and the SSR, I140, become a part of the permanent file of disapproved proposed systems. The proposed system can be reactivated by the requester after 4 months elapsed time. In that case, the process would begin at the start of Phase I.

> *Note:* The 4 months is arbitrary and should be adjusted according to corporate policy.

10. If the requester elects to appeal the DPM decision, the AD, I10, and SSR, I140, are submitted to the ISPC for review.

11. The ISPC can override the DPM decision or allow it to stand.

12. A rejection of the requester's appeal should be reflected in an interoffice memorandum from the ISPC Head (ISPCH) to the requester. The proposed system is then tabled. The AD, I10; SSR, I140; and the interoffice memorandum, appended to the SSR, become a part of the permanent file of disapproved systems. The proposed system can be resubmitted for consideration after 4 months elapsed time, in which case the process begins at the start of Phase I.

13. The ISPCH submits an SSR, I140, to the requester that reflects the approval of the proposed system and an estimated completion date (selected through ISPCH and DPM arbitration). This SSR overrides the previous SSR. The previous SSR is invalid and should be removed from the system documentation.

14. The Applications Description, I10, is sent to the ISPCH and copies are distributed to each ISPC member at least 2 weeks prior to the ISPC meeting scheduled for review of the AD. Each member should be prepared to discuss the advantages and disadvantages of the proposed system from his perspective.

After reviewing the AD the ISPC can request further information from the requester to supplement the AD. The ISPC can request further information after each review session until the AD and supplemental information are considered complete by the ISPC. To do this the ISPC compiles a memorandum to be sent to the requester that details any request for further information. The memo should include a list of questions to be addressed by the requester. Questions should be specific so that only the matter in question will be addressed in the requester reply. The requester, with the aid of a systems analyst, if required, must respond to the ISPC request by answering all questions. The written reply should be completed on a General Purpose Form, G10, and attached to the AD.

15. The ISPC reviews the AD (and supplemental information on the proposed system, if applicable) and weighs the merits of the concept and the need for the proposed system. The proposed system is either tabled as being inconsistent with the needs of the company and/or deficient in applicability, or it is accepted for further study.

16. The proposed system is tabled. The ISPCH completes the SSR, I140. The completed SSR is sent to the requester. The SSR and the AD become a part of the permanent file of disapproved proposed systems. The proposed system can be resubmitted for consideration after 4 months elapsed time, in which case the process would begin at the start of Phase I.

17. The ISPCH selects, from members of the ISPC, an ISPC liaison for the proposed system. The ISPC liaison should be an individual who will be directly affected by the implementation of the proposed system. If this is not possible, a member should be selected that is familiar with the operational functions affected by the proposed system. The Feasibility Study Team (FST) and the Project Team (PT) of Phase II interact when the ISPC is not in session.

18. The package of the proposed system documentation compiled thus far is sent to the user head(s) (UH) involved. The DPM, SC, and UH meet to assess personnel availability in their respective departments for the purpose of conducting a comprehensive feasibility study (Phase I). If it is determined that personnel are not available to begin within a reasonable period of time, the proposed system is tabled.

19. Same as described in Block 16, except that the ISPC liaison completes the SSR, I140.

20. The SC completes an SSR, I140, and submits it to the ISPC. The SSR should reflect a commitment of personnel resources (man-weeks) for both user and DP personnel and the time frame over which this commitment is valid.

21. After reviewing the personnel commitments and approving the concept and usefulness of the proposed system, the ISPC determines whether or not the proposed system merits a feasibility study (FS). The requester is asked to be present at the ISPC meeting designated for making this decision. If appropriate, the ISPCH may request that an oral presentation be given by the requester and/or the systems analyst involved.

The feasibility study involves a considerable commitment of personnel time and company money; therefore, the end result of the feasibility study should be more than a basis for determining whether or not to proceed with the implementation of the proposed system. A well-documented and thorough feasibility study serves as the framework for the actual development process. Furthermore, a comprehensive feasibility study serves to ensure that adverse surprises will be minimized during Phase II. The comprehensive feasibility study advocated in this DP Manual eliminates the need for a general system design.

22. Same as Block 19.

23. The ISPC liaison submits to the requester an SSR, I140, which reflects the go-ahead approval for a feasibility study. This SSR serves as the formal ISPC commission for a feasibility study. It should include the time frame during which the FS is to be conducted (estimated starting and completion dates). The head of the feasibility study team (FSTH) can request an extension at any time by submitting an SSR to the ISPC, should extraordinary circumstances preclude the scheduled completion of the feasibility study.

24. The Systems Coordinator (SC) appoints one or more systems analysts and the UH appoints one or more user representatives to make up the feasibility study team (FST) and conduct the feasibility study (FS). The FST should be comprised of at least one systems analyst and at least one user representative. Depending upon the scope and time frame of the FS, the FST may consist of two or more members. The user representative(s) should be well acquainted with the present system.

The FST head (FSTH) should be appointed by the SC. The head should be a systems analyst on the computer center staff. The FS is conducted under the scrutiny of the SC and the UH. The ultimate responsibility for completion of the FS rests with the Systems Coordinator.

25. If any or all of the FST members require any training in the user or DP area, sufficient time should be allotted for training and/or orientation. User personnel are responsible for training DP personnel in the application areas and vice versa.

26. The FST conducts preliminary interviews with all user personnel involved in the present system and with those who will be involved in the development and, ultimately, the use of the proposed system. At the FS stage these interviews are primarily orientation interviews that make information gathering for Phase I documentation easier and acquaint the user with approaches for conducting a feasibility study and for development. After the initial interviews, the feasibility study team will have continual contact and numerous interviews with these persons as the data gathering for the study progresses. The interviews are "as needed" and are, therefore, not included on the work flow diagram.

27. The FST completes the Definition of Proposed System, I20. The purposes of this report are to present a comprehensive word picture of the proposed system and to define all interacting operational systems (manual or automated) and significant deviations from the present mode of operation. This report ensures that all involved systems are so noted in the documentation.

28. The FST completes the System Design Constraints, I30. The purpose of this report is to detail, at the onset of the system development process, the equipment, costs, schedule, and procedural, software, and operating constraints that may limit the definition and design of the proposed system.

29. The SC and UH review the Definition of Proposed System, I20, and System Design Constraints, I30. The distribution of the reports and the coordination of the meeting, as well as subsequent review meetings, are the responsibility of the head of the FST. The head of the FST should be present during the meeting to offer assistance and clarification of the reports as required.

Each report is either approved as presented, approved conditionally pending minor revisions, or rejected. Another formal review of the report is necessary only when the report is rejected. If the report is rejected, the SC is responsible for communicating with the FSTH to relate those points in question. This communication should be both oral and written. The written communication should be in the form of an informal interoffice memo and should briefly list those points to be reevaluated and revised by the FST. This memo is destroyed after acceptance of the report.

30. It is the responsibility of the FST to reaccomplish the report(s) under the scrutiny of the SC and UH. The FST addresses those questions about the report(s) related by the SC and makes revisions as required. The distribution of the report(s) and the coordination of the follow-up meeting are the responsibility of the FSTH.

31. The FST completes the System Reports and Documents, I40, for the present system only. One purpose of this report is to ensure that all reports and documents that are part of the present system are collected, properly logged, and included in the Present System General Flowchart, I70. Another purpose is to provide a mechanism for continually logging new and old reports and documents that become a part of the proposed system. Therefore, this report will not be entirely complete until implementation of the proposed system and should be continually updated by the FST in Phase I and by the Project Team (PT) in Phase II.

32. The FST completes the System Data Files, I50. The purpose of the System Data Files report is to define and describe all data files, either manual or computer-controlled, that exist in the present system. The activity and maintenance of each of these files should be included in the Present System General Flowchart, I70.

33. The FST completes the System Data Elements, I60. The System Data Elements report is a logical composition and description of the data elements in the present system. The System Data Elements report is also used to define and describe data elements to be used in the proposed system. This report serves as a mechanism by which present and proposed data elements can be logged continually through the progression of Phases I and II. Therefore, this report will not be entirely complete until implementation of the proposed system. The report should be continually updated by the FST through Phase I and by the project team through Phase II.

34. Proceed for the System Reports and Documents, I40, System Data Files, I50, and System Data Elements, I60, as described in Block 29.

35. Same as Block 30.

36. The FST completes the Present System General Flowchart, I70. The purposes of the Present System General Flowchart are to reduce the present operational procedures to the basic component parts (input, processing, output) and to emphasize their logical relationship by using system flowcharting techniques. Proceed for the Present System General Flowchart as described in Blocks 29 and 30.

37. After reports I20, I30, I40, I50, I60, and I70 have been completed and accepted, the FSTH completes an SSR, I140, which reflects the current status of the FS and the general progress of the study.

38. The FST should query managers of companies of similar size and operation, by telephoning or by mailing a questionnaire, to determine if all or part of the system in their company, which is commensurate with the proposed system, is automated. Also, the FST should research commercial software catalogues to determine if applicable commercial packaged systems exist (see "Software Evaluation and Selection," Chapter 12). Having researched the state-of-the-art in the area of the proposed system, the FST should compile a list of all similar systems in other companies and of commercial software packages. Every entry should include the name of the company using or selling the system, address, DPM or marketing representative in charge, telephone number, and other pertinent information of a general nature.

This list is meant to be a working list only and should not be compiled to include specific operating information about any system. It is for the internal use of the FST.

39. If a similar automated system does exist, the FST should investigate the possibility of technology transfer and the extent that such a transfer could aid in the system development process; otherwise, the company should continue with in-house development of the generalized system.

40. The FST prioritizes the list of similar existing systems based on existing knowledge of the systems.

41. The FSTH contacts, by telephone, another company or a software vendor to discuss in more detail aspects of their system that relate to the proposed system.

42. Are the software and hardware compatible with existing software and hardware? If not, it is necessary to assess, in general, the required modifications to the present hardware configuration and/or software capabilities. If these modifications are deemed too extensive by the FST, this existing system should be discarded as inappropriate.

43. If the existing system is in operation at another company and marketed by the company, or if the system is available commercially, the FST must interface closely with the ISPC liaison, UH, and DPM to determine if the cost of purchasing the system is acceptable.

44. If the system is in operation at another company, the company should be asked if it is willing to cooperate by allowing FST members to visit its site and gather system and program documentation for the purpose of investigating the feasibility of technology transfer.

> *Note:* Since the investigation of technology transfer is a routine procedure, the requesting company has adopted the general policy of cooperating with other companies that make requests for technology transfers.

45. The similar system being investigated should be set aside for further study.

46. If another system exists on the list of similar existing systems, the process of determining potential for technology transfer is reinitiated.

47. If at least one viable alternative from the list of similar existing systems appears feasible and merits further investigation, then this (or these) system(s) should be studied more thoroughly by the FST at the site or via correspondence; otherwise, the FST begins the generalized system design on an in-house basis.

48. The FST selects those systems that have the greatest potential for technology transfer. The options should be given priorities with the one having the greatest potential first. As a rule of thumb, the list should be narrowed to no more than three options by this stage.

49. The FST either mails a request for system and program documentation or, if required, arranges a site visit at a time convenient for the user and DP personnel of the cooperating company, or at a commercial software distributor's demonstration location.

It is the responsibility of the FSTH to make all internal and external arrangements for the site visits.

If the FST elects to query the software suppliers by mail, this letter should simply request that the supplier send a copy of all available system and program documentation. Requesting a list of specific items should be avoided since the documentation of the existing system is probably not in the same format as that of the DP Manual; furthermore, an itemized request would dampen the spirit of cooperation.

The letter should indicate a desire to reimburse the software supplier for all copying costs.

If the FST elects to visit the site in order to gather information on the existing system, the FST should gather all available system and program documentation. Moreover, the FST should conduct interviews with both user and DP personnel. The emphasis of these interviews should be the determination of the satisfaction level of the present system and the pitfalls experienced during the course of the development of the present system.

The FSTH should follow up with a letter of appreciation to the DPM of the cooperating company after the documentation is received or the site visit is complete.

50. Have all of the options been investigated?

51. The FST relates the system documentation of the transferability options to the Phase I documentation, as applicable. The FST describes, in memorandum format (for FST internal use) for each system, the modifications required for implementation. These modifications could be in organization, in hardware, in software, in personnel, in procedures, etc.

52. From the description of required modifications, the FST evaluates the transferability options as to their applicability. A judgment is made to use all, part, or none of an existing system. The responsibility for the evaluation and for the selection of an existing system for use is solely that of the FST.

The FSTH submits a System Status Report, I140, to reflect the status of the progress of the FS and the results of the evaluation of the transferability options.

53. The general system design should be well conceived by the FST at this time; however, further user interviews should be conducted as appropriate prior to formalization of the general system design. The emphasis of these interviews should be basic input and output requirements.

54. The FST should update the System Reports and Documents, I40, the System Data Files, I50, and the System Data Elements, I60, to reflect the changes required to accommodate the proposed system.

> *Note:* If existing documentation of an existing system is to be used, then that documentation should be recompiled in the DP Manual format. If this is the case, other Phase I documentation may also require updating.

55. The FST completes the Proposed System General Flowchart, I80. The purposes of the Proposed System General Flowchart are to reduce the proposed operational procedures to the basic component parts (input, processing, output) and to emphasize their logical relationship by using system flowcharting techniques. If the original Definition of Proposed System, I20, conflicts with the system as described in the flowchart, update the I20 to reflect the most recent changes.

56. The FST completes the Scope of System Development, I90. The purpose of this report is to define the scope of the project as it relates to time frame, manpower, training, computer usage, and other information pertinent to scope definition.

57. The FST completes the Glossary of Unique Terms, I100. The purpose of this Glossary is not to present definitions of general computer technology but to define and describe those terms, abbreviations, and phrases that are peculiar to the present or proposed system. This list serves as a reference for those persons reading and preparing the documentation but not acquainted with the system. Note that the Glossary is the only noncompulsory document in Phase I; however, few systems have no unique terms, abbreviations, and/or phrases. There will usually be a Glossary.

58. The FST completes the Benefits Report, I110. The purpose of the Benefits Report is to define and describe both the tangible and intangible benefits to be derived from implementation of the proposed system. This report contains the positive justification of the development and implementation of the proposed system.

59. The FST completes the Cost Report I120. The purposes of the Cost Report are to summarize the Phase I costs, to estimate the Phase II one-time costs, and to estimate the recurring costs after implementation.

60. Proceed for the Proposed System General Flowchart, I80; Scope of System Development, I90; Glossary of Unique Terms, I100; Benefits Report, I110; and Cost Report, I120, as described in Blocks 29 and 30.

61. Same as Block 30.

62. The Feasibility Study, I130, is compiled and submitted to the ISPCH (chairman of ISPC). The Feasibility Study (minus the Technical Supplement) is distributed to each ISPC member, the DPM, and UH at least 2 weeks prior to the scheduled meeting. The ISPCH may invite to the meeting appropriate persons who can render clarification to the Feasibility Study results. The Technical Supplement is distributed to the SC for the permanent files and to others upon request.

63. The ISPC reviews the Feasibility Study. The FSTH presents a brief oral summary of the proposed system at the ISPC meeting and entertains questions from the members. The ISPC directs that the project be either tabled indefinitely, approved and given the go-ahead to proceed to Phase II, or approved but placed in a queue of approved systems in the appropriate priority position. The ISPC should make a decision and report their decision to the requester within 6 weeks after the ISPCH receives the Feasibility Study. Note that more than one ISPC meeting can be scheduled to review the Summary Report.

> *Note:* When accepting a cost report, the ISPC is also accepting the possibility of a 12% cost overrun.

64. The proposed system is rejected by the ISPC and is tabled indefinitely. The ISPC Liaison is responsible for formally notifying the requester of the ISPC decision to reject the project. The notification is in the form of an SSR, I140, and is submitted to the requester. The entire Feasibility Study and all SSR's become a part of the permanent file of rejected systems. The proposed system documentation can be resubmitted for consideration by the ISPC after 4 months elapsed time.

65. The proposed system is approved for development but is given less than top priority. The ISPC places the approved proposed system in the appropriate priority position in a queue of approved systems. The ISPC Liaison informs the requester via an SSR, I140, of the approval, priority position, and the approximate date on which the requester can expect Phase II to begin.

66. The ISPC periodically reviews the list of approved systems. The ISPC may elect to rearrange the priorities according to current needs of the company. The ISPC may elect to initiate Phase II of system development for one or more of the proposed systems or simply take no action at all.

67. The proposed system is approved and given an unconditional go-ahead to Phase II. The ISPC Liaison informs the requestor via an SSR, I140, of the approval and Phase II initiation.

Documentation Instructions and Forms—Phase 1

APPLICATIONS DESCRIPTION—I10

Instructions

Form: General Purpose, G10.
Responsibility: Requester.

> *Note:* The Requester, if user, may request assistance from the Computer Center. The SC will then designate a systems analyst to assist the user in the preparation of the Applications Description.

Content: The Applications Description (AD) is a general narrative description of the proposed system in nontechnical terms that can be easily understood by non-DP personnel. It should not exceed seven typewritten, double-spaced pages on the form G10 and should include:

1. Title of system. Title should be descriptive of the system, but brief. Use existing titles when applicable.
2. System identification. A two alpha character identifier assigned by the Computer Center.
3. Date. Date of completion of the AD.
4. Prepared by. Include (a) names, (b) positions, and (c) affiliations.
5. General description of system. Include:
   - *a.* Statement of objectives for the proposed system
   - *b.* A general word picture of the fundamental operation of the proposed system
   - *c.* Scope of proposed system covering all organizational interfaces, volumes and frequencies of activity, complexity of system, programming, data base development, and personnel requirements.
6. Present system's problems. Identify problem areas in the present system or the present mode of operation. Be candid and explicit.
7. Justification. Specify how the proposed system will solve present problems, increase services, upgrade management reporting, save money, etc.
8. Funding source. Identify source(s) of funds that will provide the funding for development.
9. Time frame. Expected starting date and expected completion date.

Note: If timing is critical, include an explanation.

10. Applicable documents. Identify documents which contain pertinent information (e.g., policy statements issued by top management, directives, general policy, departmental policies and procedures, and any operational procedures).
11. Similar successful systems. If applicable, examples of successful systems in other companies should be cited. Name company(ies), and department or division head(s) responsible for the similar system. Include telephone numbers if available. If the cooperating department head(s) has benefit/cost data on the operational system, include this in Applications Description.
12. Long-range objectives of proposed system, such as augmentation and/or future interface with a proposed and/or an existing system.
13. Other pertinent information.

DEFINITION OF PROPOSED SYSTEM—I20

Instructions

Form: General Purpose, G10.

Responsibility: Feasibility Study Team Head (FSTH).

Content: The purpose of the Definition of Proposed System is to provide a word picture of the operation of the proposed system. Also, this report serves to establish a base for the feasibility study and to provide management with an overview of the proposed system. It includes:

1. Word picture of proposed system. Describe in nontechnical terms the fundamental operations of the proposed system. Include the present systems (manual or automated) with which the proposed system must be compatible and/or dependent and describe the relationship between the systems. This should be a more detailed description than the general word picture of the Applications Description, I10.
2. Significant differences. Enumerate those procedures, approaches, and/or methods that are expected to deviate considerably from the present mode of operation.

Note: This report should be accomplished with as much detail as possible in order to provide a common ground for the feasibility study. Also, this report should be completely reworked after the proposed system is solidified or after each major design modification. Reference the Proposed System General Flowchart as backup to I20 when it is complete.

SYSTEM DESIGN CONSTRAINTS—I30

Instructions

Form: General Purpose, G10.

Responsibility: Feasibility Study Team Head.

Content: The proposed system will be developed subject to specific constraints. These constraints may limit the definition and design of the proposed system. Address the constraints according to the following categories.

1. Equipment constraints. The system must be designed within the limits of the available equipment or provisions must be made to upgrade the present equipment.
2. Cost constraints. Any developmental, operational, or maintenance cost limitations.
3. Schedule constraints. Computer availability, implementation dates, corporate cycles, etc. Provide an explanation of schedule constraints.
4. Procedural constraints. Any limitation on the sequence in which existing functions are performed or degree of standardization required by existing policy.
5. Software constraints. Requirement to use existing applications and/or systems software or unavailability of commercial software.
6. Operating constraints. These constraints generally relate to system reliability (MTBF, MTTR), accuracy, response and/or turnaround time, capacity, frequency, flexibility, and costs.
7. Other constraints. List and describe other pertinent constraints.

SYSTEM REPORTS AND DOCUMENTS—I40

Instructions

Form: I40.

Responsibility: Feasibility Study Team Head.

Content: The reports and documents are listed for both the present and proposed systems. Note that all reports and documents for the proposed system may not be known when defining the present system and should be included in the list as the system development process progresses through Phases I and II.

1. Number. Assign each report/document a number for cross-reference to attached sample copies.
2. Title. List the titles of all reports and documents (any standard communication or form) either present or proposed, either computer produced or manually produced. The I40 should ultimately be a comprehensive list of all hard copy I/O in both the present and proposed systems.

Numbers 3, 4, 5, and 6 refer to a report or document. Mark only one for each title.

3. Present. Mark "X" in block if presently used and will be retained in its present format in the proposed system.
4. Proposed. Mark "X" in block if not presently used but will be used in the proposed system.
5. Presently used, to be revised. Mark "X" in block if presently used but will be revised for use in the proposed system (e.g., reformatting and/or minor additions or deletions).
6. Presently used, to be deleted. Mark "X" in block if presently used but will be deleted and no longer maintained in the proposed system.
7. Cycle (e.g., daily, weekly, etc.). If no cycle, put "NA," or "on demand" if applicable.
8. Distribution. List distribution by agency name(s) and/or title(s) or position(s) of personnel, if applicable. Use as many lines as required, then list the next report or document on the next complete line.

9. Total number of pages of Form I40 used.
10. Page number.
11. Attach sample copies of existing reports and documents and others as they become available. Place the appropriate assigned number in the upper righthand corner of each sample report or document.

REPORT TITLE SYSTEM REPORTS AND DOCUMENTS	NO. I40	DATE
SYSTEM TITLE		ID

dpm

NO.	TITLE	PRESENT	PROPOSED	TO BE REVISED	TO BE DELETED	CYCLE	DISTRIBUTION
(1)	(2)	(3)	(4)	(5)	(6)	(7)	(8)

PAGE (10)/(9)

SYSTEM DATA FILES—I50

Instructions

Form: I50.

Responsibility: Feasibility Study Team Head.

Content: The System Data Files form is used to identify, in general, the pertinent manual or automated files in the present system and those expected to be maintained in the proposed system. The following information should be included on or with a separate I50 form for each data file.

1. Name of file. If no name exists, select a brief descriptive title for the file (or data base, if appropriate).
2. Responsibility. Division and/or department responsible for maintaining the file. If the file is automated, name the primary user.
3. Storage medium. Indicate how the file is stored—file cabinet in manila folder, magnetic disk, magnetic tape, 3 × 5 inch cards, kardex, etc.
4. Storage scheme. Include name of logical record and method of storage (e.g., the employee record is stored by social security number in an ascending sequence).

Numbers 5, 6, 7, and 8 refer to the file. Mark only one of the four.

5. Present. Mark "X" in block if presently used and will be retained in its present format in the proposed system.
6. Proposed. Mark "X" in block if not used presently but will be used in the proposed system.
7. Presently used, to be revised. Mark "X" in block if presently used but will be revised for use in the proposed system. If the revision is in storage medium, indicate "to be deleted" and complete another I50 with a "proposed" indication.
8. Presently used, to be deleted. Mark "X" in block if presently used but will be deleted and no longer maintained in the proposed system.
9. Provide, in paragraph format, a brief but complete description of the contents of the file.

10. Total number of pages of Form I50 used.

11. Page number.

12. Attach a copy of the preprinted form, record description, or a copy of a representative record that contains all of the entries.

REPORT TITLE	SYSTEM DATA FILES	NO. I50	DATE
SYSTEM TITLE			ID

File Name:	(1)	Present	(5)
Responsibility:	(2)	Proposed	(6)
Storage Medium:	(3)	To Be Revised	(7)
Storage Scheme:	(4)	To Be Deleted	(8)

(9)

PAGE (11) / (10)

SYSTEM DATA ELEMENTS—I60

Instructions

Form: I60.

Responsibility: Feasibility Study Team Head, Phase I;
Project Team Head, Phase II.

Content: The data elements are listed for both the present and proposed systems. Note that data elements for the proposed system may not be known when describing the present system and should be included as the design progresses through Phases I and II.

1. Data element number. To be added after completion of the Data Element Matrix Report, II350, of Phase II. The number should correspond to the number listed on the Data Element Matrix.
2. Title. A brief descriptive title for the data element (e.g., employee ID).
3. Description. Use any number of lines up to three to write an expanded description of the data element. Note that some titles may be self-explanatory and further description is not required. Descriptions which require more space should be included in the Glossary, I100, under the data element's title. In such a case, put "see Glossary" under description.

Numbers 4, 5, 6, and 7 refer to a data element. Mark only one for each data element.

4. Present. Mark "X" in block if presently used and will be retained in its present format in the proposed system.
5. Proposed. Mark "X" in block if not used presently but will be used in proposed system.
6. Presently used, to be revised. Mark "X" in block if presently used but will be revised for use in the proposed system (e.g., account number coding scheme increased from five to seven characters).
7. Presently used, to be deleted. Mark "X" in block if presently used but will be deleted and no longer maintained in the proposed system.
8. Update requirements. Put daily, weekly, monthly random, etc., as required.

9. Source. Describe source (agency, document, system, person, etc.). If the source needs explanation, abbreviate and attach a legend with the explanation.
10. Responsibility. Name of agency and/or title of person responsible for update. This item is not required after completion of the Data Element Matrix, II350. Even when the data element is maintained on an automated medium in the Computer Center, the responsibility still resides with the primary user.
11. Total number of pages of Form I60.
12. Page number.

REPORT TITLE SYSTEM DATA ELEMENTS	NO. 160	DATE
SYSTEM TITLE		ID

dpm

NO.	TITLE	DESCRIPTION	PRESENT	PROPOSED	TO BE REVISED	TO BE DELETED	UPDATE REQUIREMENT	SOURCE	RESPONSIBILITY
(1)	(2)	(3)	(4)	(5)	(6)	(7)	(8)	(9)	(10)

PAGE (12) / (11)

PRESENT SYSTEM GENERAL FLOWCHART—I70

Instructions

Forms: Flowchart Form, G20; General Purpose Form, G10.

Responsibility: Feasibility Study Team Head.

Content: The purposes of the Present System General Flowchart are to reduce the present operational procedures to the basic component parts (input, processing, output) and to emphasize their logical relationships by using system flowcharting techniques. The flowchart should provide a general description of the information and work flow of the present system (emphasizing the elements within the system that control work flow). If such a flowchart does not already exist within the company structure, one should be developed and should be on file whether the proposed system is implemented or not. The flowchart will be a by-product of the feasibility study and will be a valuable aid for future interrelated systems developments.

1. Use standard systems flowchart symbols (see II400).
2. Show all reports and documents (from System Reports and Documents, I40) and files and/or data bases in their proper relationship to one another.
3. Show manual or computer processes in the proper sequence. The flowchart can be organized and presented in a variety of methods. Select that which is most applicable (e.g., hierarchical, by subsystem activated by random events, by function, by minor and major cycles, by subsystems, or a combination thereof). Few systems can be in straight sequential order. A modular approach is applicable in most cases.
4. Use the General Purpose form, G10, to explain the organization and presentation of the flowchart if other than simple sequential. Also use the G10 form where supplemental description is necessary to fully explain an operation, report, file usage, departmental interface, etc.
5. Use Decision Tables, II410 and II420, to supplement the flowchart logic if necessary.

PROPOSED SYSTEM GENERAL FLOWCHART—I80

Instructions

Forms: Flowchart Form, G20; General Purpose Form, G10.

Responsibility: Feasibility Study Team Head.

Content: The purposes of the Proposed System General Flowchart are to reduce the proposed system procedures to their component parts and to emphasize their logical relationships by using system flowcharting techniques. The flowchart should be specific enough to: serve as an outline for suggesting alternative approaches to system development, serve as a guideline for a detailed flowchart in Phase II, and enable the analyst to make a reasonable benefit/cost analysis of the proposed system. The general flowchart need not be so specific as to reduce the system to its most basic components. This is accomplished in Phase II.

1. Use standard systems flowchart symbols (see II400).
2. Show all reports and documents (from System Reports and Documents, I40) and files and/or data bases in their proper relationship to one another.
3. Show manual or computer processes in the proper sequence. The flowchart can be organized and presented in a variety of methods. Select that which is most applicable (e.g., hierarchical, by subsystem activated by random events, by function, by minor and major cycles, by subsystems, or a combination thereof). Few systems can be in straight sequential order. A modular approach is applicable in most cases.
4. Use the General Purpose form, G10, to explain the organization and presentation of the flowchart if other than simple sequential. Also use the G10 form where supplemental description is necessary to fully explain an operation, report, file usage, departmental interface, etc.
5. Use Decision Tables, II410 and II420, to supplement the flowchart logic if necessary.
6. If the original Definition of Proposed System, I20, conflicts with the system as described in the flowchart, update the I20 to reflect the most recent changes.

SCOPE OF SYSTEM DEVELOPMENT—I90

Instructions

Form: General Purpose, G10.

Responsibility: Feasibility Study Team Head.

Content: After having assessed the degree of complexity of the proposed system by preparing a Proposed System General Flowchart, it is necessary to define the scope of the system development process. Include:

1. The expected duration of Phase I and Phase II (Parts 1, 2, and 3). Make an optimistic, a pessimistic, and a most likely estimate for the duration of each of the above four stages of system development.
2. Manpower requirements for users, DP and others. Describe by position title and estimated man-weeks.
3. Training requirements for users, DP and others. Define general area of training, who receives the training, the duration of training, and who administers the training.
4. Machine time required. Indicate location and availability of computer, if other than that of the general Computer Center.
5. Other pertinent information.

GLOSSARY OF UNIQUE TERMS—I100

Instructions

Form: General Purpose, G10.

Responsibility: Feasibility Study Team Head.

Content: In the course of describing any system, there are usually certain terms and/or phrases peculiar to that system and not familiar to all users, ISPC, DP personnel, etc. It is therefore necessary to list and define these terms as a reference for persons not acquainted with the system. This list also precludes the requirement to define these terms each time they are included in a report. Do not include technical data processing terms.

1. List unique terms and/or phrases in alphabetical order.
2. Definitions should be descriptive and in nontechnical terms.
3. This form should be updated throughout Phases I, II, and III, as required.

BENEFITS REPORT—I110

Instructions

Form: General Purpose, G10.

Responsibility: Feasibility Study Team Head.

Content: The purpose of the Benefits Report is to define and describe both the tangible and intangible benefits to be derived from implementation of the proposed system. This report comprises the positive justification for development and implementation of the proposed system. The analysis should include:

1. All direct and indirect savings in manpower and/or resources. Associate all savings with a specific budget center. Make an estimate of expected monetary savings for each reduction in manpower or resource requirements (e.g., 1.5 man-weeks of secretarial time per month, $150/month, Department of Finance, Accounting Division; 3 hours machine time per month, $200/month, Computer Center).
2. A comprehensive list of intangible benefits (e.g., increased service, fewer errors on invoices, faster turnaround, etc.). Provide a detailed explanation of each intangible benefit. (For example, explain benefits derived from faster turnaround.)

Note: Certain intangible benefits may result indirectly in dollar savings. The indirect savings should be included in the "total dollar savings" below.

3. Total dollar savings. Summary of all expected monetary savings presented by budget year.

COST REPORT—I120

Instructions

Form: I120.

Responsibility: Feasibility Study Team Head.

Content: The Cost Report is a summary of all costs of the feasibility study (Phase I); the estimated costs of design, development, and implementation (Phase II); and the monthly recurring costs after implementation (Phase III). The costs are presented by phase for each budget center. The total cost to the company (costs to all budget centers) is matched against the total savings (from the Benefits Report, I110) to get the net cost to the company.

Note: All costs presented in the Cost Report are absolute dollar costs to the company. For example, if an assistant user manager works 5 hours per week on the project and still accomplishes his basic job function, there is no cost to the company. If a systems analyst works full time on the project and her time is charged to the Planning Department, this cost is to the company since the systems analyst could have been assigned to another project. Also, if the system testing, or even operation, utilizes unused computer capacity, no costs should be reflected on the Cost Report; however, if system testing or operation requires an increase of 128K words of primary storage, then the costs should be reflected in the Cost Report.

1. Budget center. A cost report is completed for each budget center involved. Place the name of the budget center here (e.g., Planning Department). The last page of Form I120 will always be a summary of all costs and should be marked "Summary." See items 8, 17, 18, and 19.
2. Labor. Break labor costs down by appropriate positions [e.g., Management (user), Management (DP), systems analysts, programmers, operators, data entry, specific operational user personnel, etc.] and list the titles in the spaces provided. A titled entry may represent more than one person (e.g., six systems analysts).

Note: The total number of man-days involved for a particular position can be reflected in parentheses by the associated cost figure [e.g., $480.00 (3)]. This entry is optional.

Note: "Labor" refers to work directly related to system development and operation.

3. Materials and equipment—User. Actual and/or expected costs to the user of all nonreusable physical material, additional computer hardware and/or software, and supplemental equipment. Include an itemized list in the Cost Report Appendix if necessary.
4. Materials and equipment—Computer Center. Actual and/or expected costs to the Computer Center for materials and equipment. See 3 above.
5. Travel. Per diem.
6. Travel. Transportation.
7. Miscellaneous. Miscellaneous should include all items that cannot be classified as labor, materials and equipment, or travel. List miscellaneous cost items in the space provided. For example, the cost of remodeling the machine room to accommodate new equipment should be placed under miscellaneous costs.
8. Budget center. The budget center of the first sheet will be listed on the first line and so on. List only one budget center per Form I120 except on the last sheet, which summarizes all costs from all budget centers.

   The costs are presented relative to a particular budget center and on a separate Form I120. All Form I120's will have only one budget center listed in its respective position except the last Form I120. The last Form I120 (titled "Summary" in item one above) contains a summary of costs by phase. Do this by listing all applicable budget centers and their associated costs by phase.
9. Actual cost—Phase I. Costs reflected in this column are actual costs incurred during Phase I. The "Budget Center" line is the total of the itemized costs for a particular budget center.
10. Estimated cost—Phase II. During the initial preparation and subsequent Cost Report updates, estimated costs for Phase II would be reflected in this column.
11. Actual cost—Phase II. Upon completion of Phase II, reflect the actual costs incurred.
12. Budget year. Note applicable budget year (e.g., '79 for calendar year or '79–'80 for split or fiscal budget years).

13, 14, 15, 16. Estimated Monthly Recurring Costs. Reflect over a 4-year horizon the average estimated monthly recurring costs of system operation for each of up to 4 years (2 years minimum). Itemized monthly costs may be included in the Cost Report Appendix if needed.

17. Total cost. Total of all budget center costs for each column. For the Form I120's reflecting costs of a single budget center, the budget center cost and the total cost will be the same.

18. Savings—I110. Direct and indirect monetary savings from the Benefits Report, I110. Reflect the savings for a particular budget center on the appropriate Form I120.

19. Net cost. Subtract the "savings" from total cost to get the net cost. If the net cost is negative, enclose the figure in parentheses [e.g., —$13,420 would be ($13,420)].

17,18,19. Summary cost data (Cost Report "Summary" only). The total cost should be the sum of all of the individual budget center costs. The "savings" should be the sum of all direct and indirect savings (by phase) from the Benefits Report.

20. Total number of pages of the Cost Report.

21. Page number.

Note: Some Cost Reports may require more detailed costs and explanations in order to clarify certain entries on the Cost Report. Use a General Purpose Form, G10, and label it Cost Report Appendix. Append the Cost Report Appendix to the Cost Report.

REPORT TITLE COST REPORT	NO. I120	DATE
SYSTEM TITLE		ID

Budget Center ______(1)______

	Cost Item	Phase I	Phase II		Phase III – Estimated Monthly Recurring Costs			
		Actual Cost	Estimated Cost	Actual Cost	Year 1 (12)	Year 2	Year 3	Year 4
Labor								
	(2)	(9)	(10)	(11)	(13)	(14)	(15)	(16)
Mat.& Eq.	User (3)							
	Computer Center (4)							
Travel	Per diem (5)							
	Transportation (6)							
Miscellaneous								
	(7)							
Budget Center								
	(8)							
Total Cost		(17)						
Savings – I110		(18)						
Net Cost		(19)						

PAGE (21)/(20)

FEASIBILITY STUDY COVER—I130

Instructions

Form: I130.

Responsibility: Feasibility Study Team Head.

Content: This report is the cover for the Feasibility Study. The cover lists all reports of the Feasibility Study plus a Technical Supplement. The Feasibility Study contains the reports necessary for the ISPC to make an informed "go/no-go" decision. The Technical Supplement contains the background information required for preparation of the Feasibility Study. The Technical Supplement need not be submitted to the ISPC except on request. The Technical Supplement provides the framework for the detail design of the system, Phase II.

The following information should be included on the Feasibility Study Cover:

1. Feasibility Study Team. Names, agency affiliations, and titles of members of the FST. List FSTH first.
2. ISPC liaison. Name, agency affiliation, and title.
3. Check each report included in the Feasibility Study and Technical Supplement with an "X." The Glossary, I100, is the only report that is not mandatory.

REPORT TITLE Feasibility Study Cover	No. I130	DATE
SYSTEM TITLE		ID

Feasibility Study Team

(1)

ISPC Liaison

(2)

Feasibility Study

(3)	I10	Application Description
	I20	Definition of Proposed System
	I30	System Design Constraints
	I90	Scope of System Development
	I110	Benefits Report
	I120	Cost Report
	I100	Glossary of Unique Terms

Technical Supplement

(3)	I40	System Reports and Documents
	I50	System Data Files
	I60	System Data Elements
	I70	Present System General Flowchart
	I80	Proposed System General Flowchart

SYSTEM STATUS REPORT (SSR)—I140

Instructions

Form: General Purpose, G10.

Responsibility: As defined in the Block Descriptions.

Content: The System Status Report is a multipurpose document that is used by several persons to report the status of a request for DP service, the feasibility study, the system development process, or the evaluation of an operational system. The SSR is used throughout Phases I, II, and III, as a vehicle for reporting acceptance or rejection of a proposed system or for reporting progress towards implementation of the system. All SSR's become part of the system documentation and are filed on top of the latest SSR.

The following information should be included on all SSR's:

1. Phase and block number of the work flow diagram for which the SSR is applicable.
2. Sent to. Name, agency affiliation, and title or position in the system development process (e.g., SC).
3. Prepared by. Name, agency affiliation, and title or position in the system development process.
4. Date of preparation.

For a statement of acceptance or rejection include the following:

1. A statement concerning the rejection or approval of a proposed system. There are no conditional approvals since the system development process is designed to accommodate continuous review and revision prior to the decision point.
2. If rejected, the reason for rejection of the proposed system (optional).
3. If approved, the priority relative to other approved systems. An expected date of Phase II initiation is optional.

For a statement of progress the following should be included:

1. Elapsed time, in calendar days, since the last SSR.
2. Word picture of overall project progress.

3. Description of extraordinary problems that have caused or are expected to cause delays in progress, if applicable.
4. Other pertinent information.

5

Phase II—System Analysis, Design, Programming, Conversion, and Implementation

Part 1—System Analysis and Design

Work Flow Diagrams—Phase II, Part 1

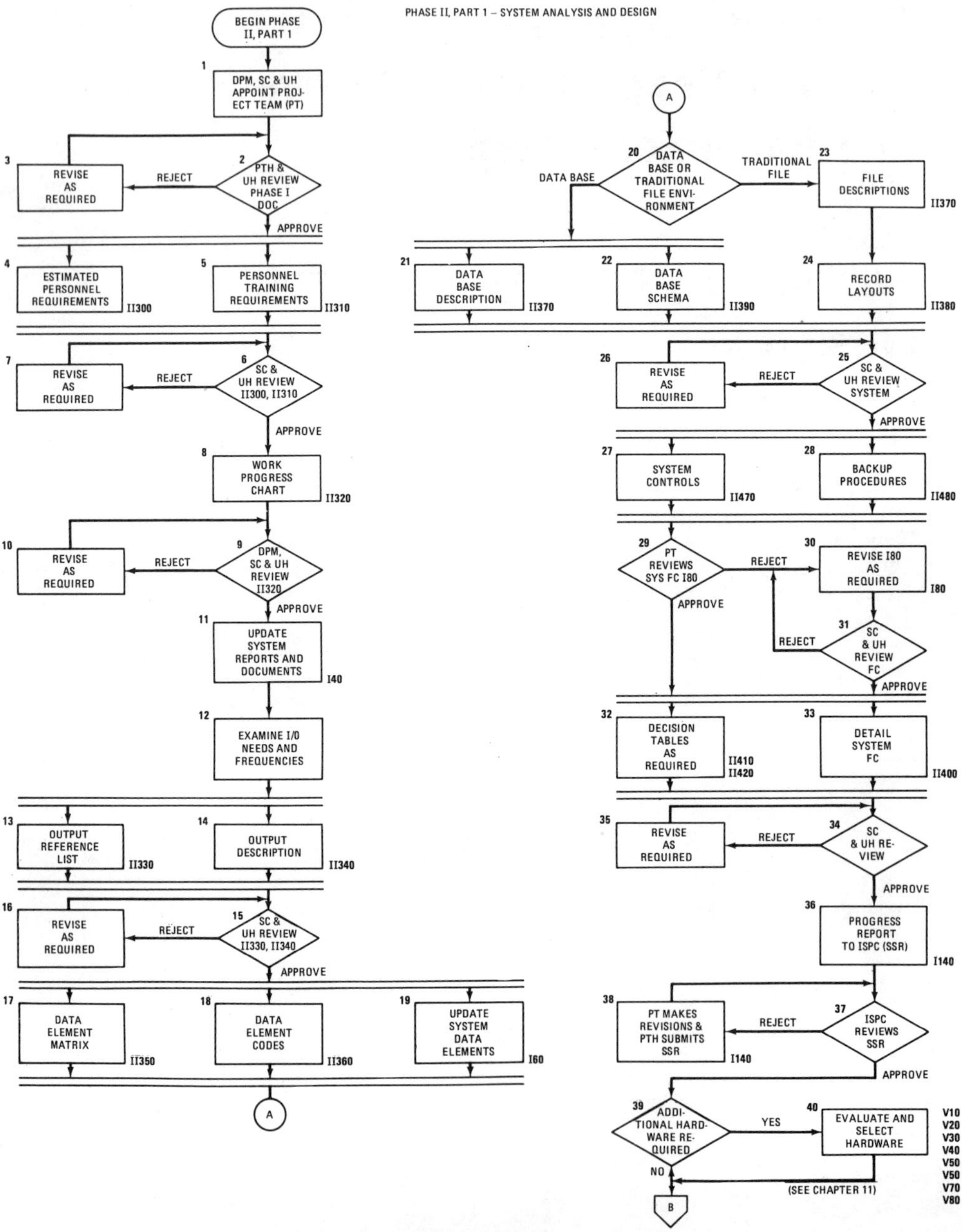

PHASE II, PART 1 – SYSTEM ANALYSIS AND DESIGN
(continued)

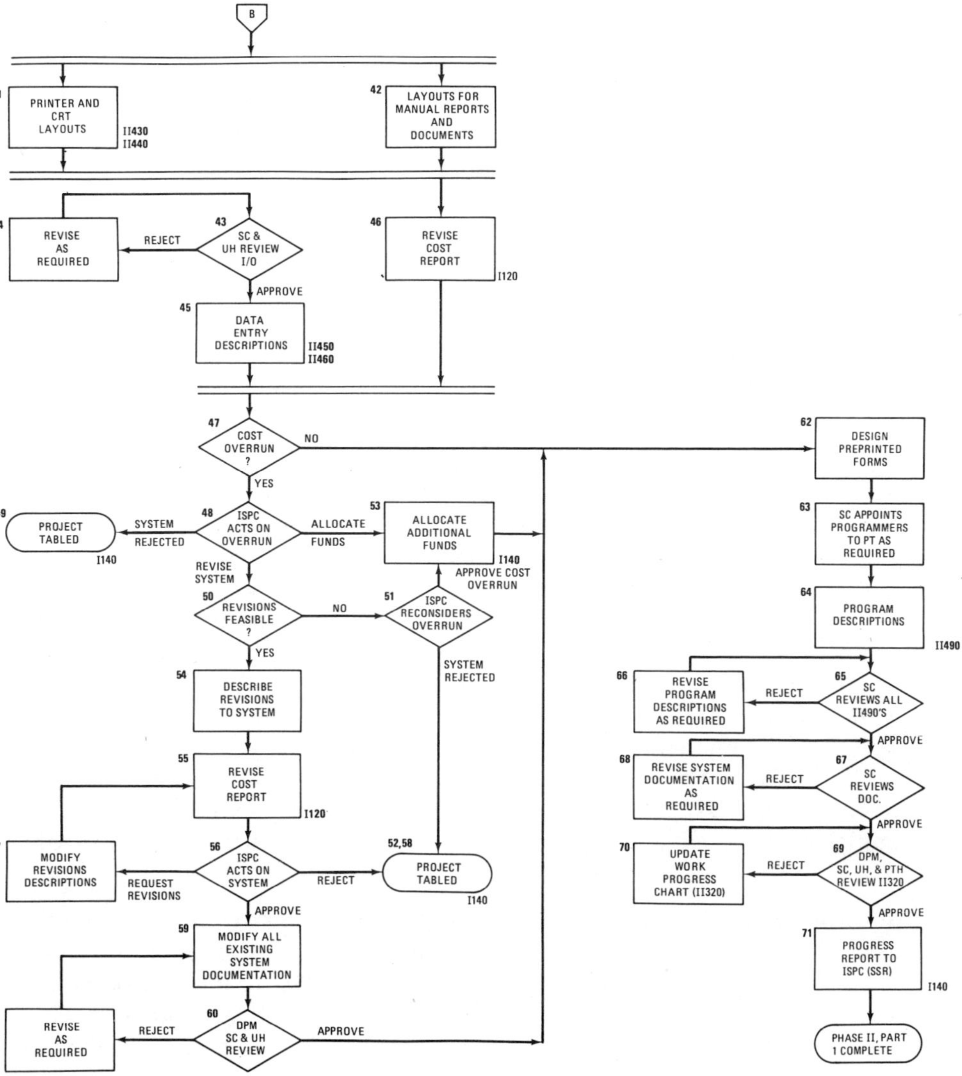

Block Descriptions—Phase II, Part 1

1. The Data Processing Manager (DPM), Systems Coordinator (SC), and user head(s) (UH) (references to UH include all heads of departments, divisions, and/or agencies that are included in the proposed system) meet to appoint the members of the Project Team (PT). Included on the team should be one or more systems analysts and one or more representatives from each department, division, and/or agency involved. At the discretion of the SC, one or more programmers may be appointed (programmers selected later in Phase II, Part 1). Other personnel may be appointed as appropriate.

The members of the FST do not necessarily become members of the PT. However, it is advisable to appoint FST members if possible. If this is not possible, FST members should work closely with PT members during the review of the Feasibility Study and the Technical Supplement.

The SC also appoints a Project Team Head (PTH). It is recommended that the PTH be a systems analyst, but it is not required. The PTH is entirely responsible for the internal organization of the PT. The PTH has the authority to organize the team in the way he feels will best accomplish the PT's objectives. This internal organization may involve an assistant PTH, subteams, and subteam leaders. The requirements for a formal internal organization depend on the size and complexity of the project.

2. The project team members and the UH familiarize themselves with the Phase I documentation contained in the Feasibility Study and Technical Supplement. Once all PT members and users become familiar with the existing and proposed systems through individual and group study of available documentation, the PTH arranges a meeting. The objectives of this meeting are to ensure that the present and proposed system documentation is correct as defined in the Phase I documentation and that the PT members and UH fully understand the Phase I documentation.

If the Phase I documentation is deemed in need of revision after review by the PT and UH, the Phase I documentation is temporarily rejected and the PT makes the necessary revisions. If the Phase I documentation is current and correct, it is accepted.

3. Any or all of the Phase I documentation should be revised to correctly reflect the status and definition of both the present and proposed systems. Once all revisions are complete, the PTH again arranges a meeting of the PT and UH to review the revisions made to the Phase I documentation. This cycle of revision and review is continued until all Phase I documentation is up to date.

4. The PT completes the Estimated Personnel Requirements, II300. The purpose of this report is to detail all personnel requirements for Phase II.

5. The PT completes the Personnel Training Requirements, II310. This

report is a record of the training required for individuals and/or groups that will be involved in the system development process and system operation.

6. Proceed for the Estimated Personnel Requirements, II300, and Personnel Training Requirements, II310 as described in Block 29 of Phase I.

Note that managers of all personnel listed in either report are asked to review the report. Each (SC or UH) can either accept or reject that portion of the report(s) involving personnel he or she supervises. Once a manager accepts, it is implied that he or she has formally made the personnel commitment noted in the report(s). If any manager rejects the report(s), the report(s), and perhaps the scope of the system, must be revised until all managers accept the report(s).

7. The PT modifies the Estimated Personnel Requirements, II300, and Personnel Training Requirements, II310, in order to accommodate the desires of the managers. The PTH should inform all managers of the effect of decreased user commitment on completion of the project, if appropriate.

8. The PT completes the Work Progress Chart, II320. The general scope of the project was defined in Phase I, and the various department heads defined the extent of involvement of their personnel. Knowing the scope of and personnel commitments to the project, the PT can make reasonable estimates of the project time schedule and thereby complete the Work Progress Chart.

9. The DPM, SC, and UH meet to review the Work Progress Chart. Their primary objective is to assess the feasibility of the time schedule depicted in the chart. The chart should be examined by each manager to ensure that times of peak work loads in the system development process and in the routine activities of the involved departments do not overlap. Regular departmental schedules should be examined for personnel and/or resource conflicts.

If it is determined that conflicts do exist, then the Work Progress Chart is returned to the PT with appropriate comments attached. The PT makes the necessary revisions and resubmits the Work Progress Chart.

If the Work Progress Chart is approved as is, then no changes are required and the Phase II time schedule is official. Once approved, the Work Progress Chart is maintained by the PTH.

10. The PT modifies the Work Progress Chart to accommodate the changes requested by the DPM, SC, and UH. The chart is then resubmitted to the DPM, SC, and UH for review.

11. The PT updates the System Reports and Documents, I40, if necessary, to include those forms, documents, reports, standard memorandums, etc., that are part of the present system and those that are to become part of the proposed system. The list should be all-inclusive to ensure that each item is properly scrutinized during the ensuing activities.

12. The PT evaluates the need and worth of each input to and output from the system, whether manual or computer produced. Each user and/or producer of the various reports, documents, forms, etc. (listed in I40) should be interviewed to obtain evaluations and details of usage. A PT member may be required to physically trace a report from its source to its permanent file. Each input or output is usually expensive to produce and often more expensive to maintain; therefore, the PT needs to evaluate each on its individual merits and recommend continuance, revision, or elimination to the UH responsible.

Also, the PT should evaluate the cycle and time frame for all inputs and outputs. For example, if a weekly status report would suffice, there is no need for a daily status report. Plan cyclic inputs and outputs so that the frequency-versus-worth trade-off is optimized. For on-line systems, check response time requirements to see if they are too stringent and also check system uptime against need.

The PT is responsible for changes made to the various system inputs and outputs. Duplication should be eliminated when possible. Incorporate similar inputs and/or outputs when possible. Eliminate information that is not required on a given input or output. Reduce operating hours and/or relax response time requirements if this can be done without affecting system operation.

13. The PT prepares the Output Reference List, II330. The list consists of all outputs produced on card, CRT, or printer. This list should be updated as the system development process progresses to include references to Output Descriptions, II340, and Layouts (II380, card; II430, printer; and II440, CRT).

14. The PT completes all Output Descriptions, II340. The purpose of each Output Description is to describe the computer-produced system output, which is either a transaction or a report. These descriptions should be updated as required.

15. The SC and UH review the Output Descriptions for completeness and accuracy. Each is individually reviewed and either rejected or accepted. When rejected, the Output Description is returned to the PT for revision. When accepted, its completion should be properly logged on the Output Reference List, II330.

16. The PT modifies the Output Descriptions, II340, as required and resubmits them to the scrutiny of the SC and UH.

17. The PT completes the Data Element Matrix, II350. The purpose of completing this report is to define all data elements that are part of the system. It is imperative that both user and DP personnel work together to ensure that the Data Element Matrix is comprehensive. The elements are defined by title, description, and required programming specifics, and by source document, reports, files, and/or data bases in which they appear.

This report should be updated as required. Data elements may be deleted or added during Phase II, Part 1, and programming specifics may become known during Phase II, Part 2.

18. The PT completes the Data Element Codes, II360, for each data element that uses a coding scheme. Each of these reports should be updated throughout the system development process as information becomes known.

When a report is completed, the appropriate page number should be included in the "code" box of the corresponding data element on the Data Element Matrix, II350. All Data Element Codes forms should then be appended to the Data Element Matrix.

19. Once all data elements are defined (at least, at this stage in the process), the System Data Elements report, I60, should be updated. The contents of this report, when updated, indicate the status of a particular data element—whether presently used, proposed, presently used but to be revised, or presently used but to be deleted. This report should be maintained throughout Phase II.

20. If data base management system (DBMS) software is used, traditional file descriptions and record layouts are not required.

21. The PT completes the Data Base Description, II370, as required. The purposes of the Data Base Description are to define the Data Base environment and to indicate logical groups of data elements on the data base. If a data base administrator exists and is not on the project team, the PTH should cooperate with the data base administrator in the completion of II370 and II390 below.

22. The PT completes the Data Base Schema, II390. The purpose of the Data Base Schema is to provide a graphical representation of the logical structure of the data base.

23. The PT completes the File Descriptions, II370, as required. The purposes of the File Description are to define the type and use of a file and to list the data elements associated with the file. This report pertains to both manual and computer maintained files.

24. The PT completes all required Record Layouts, II380. A Form II380 is completed for each File Description, II370. Each Form II380 graphically illustrates the relationship between fields, the field formats, and the field lengths.

25. The PTH calls a meeting of the SC and the UH to review all available Phase I and II documentation. The documentation should be submitted to each by the PTH at least 1 week prior to the meeting date. This meeting is very important to the ultimate success of the system. All documentation required for a detailed flowchart should have been compiled by the PT. The UH should carefully review the output generated, required input, cycle times, files, general system controls, and personnel requirements. The SC should review carefully the documentation pertinent to defining the computer center's role in the system, such as backup, hardware and software requirements, turnaround, personnel requirements, etc.

The UH and SC either accept or reject any part of or all of the documentation. Certain trade-offs may become apparent and in such cases should be arbitrated by the PTH. The SC and UH should each prepare an interoffice memorandum that reflects acceptance and/or rejection. These memos are sent to the PTH. If the memorandums reject the documentation, they should be specific and include questions to be addressed and changes to be made.

26. The PT makes the changes in the system documentation agreed upon by the SC, UH, and PTH. The documentation is then resubmitted to the SC and UH for review.

27. The PT completes the System Controls report, II470. The purpose of the System Controls report is to identify and describe all system controls (manual and/or computer) that are used to ensure the accuracy, reliability, and integrity of the system. Descriptions for physical and administrative controls, input, output, and other controls within the scope of the system are included.

28. The PT completes the Backup Procedures, II480. The purpose of this report is to define the backup and checkpoint/restart procedures in case of system failure. These procedures are described for system failures at various times during the operating cycle, as appropriate, for cyclic applications. This report may be completed, in general, prior to completion of the Detail System Flowchart, II400. The Backup Procedures should be updated to include specific details after the completion of the Detail System Flowchart. A further update might be required after programming (Phase II, Part 2).

29. The PT reviews the previously completed Proposed System General Flowchart, I80, for adherence to the specifications of the system design. Also, the PT should examine the general sequence of activities and flow of information for efficient use of information, personnel, and equipment. The PT should evaluate the system again to ensure that the system will be effective in meeting predetermined objectives. The Proposed System General Flowchart is either approved or is rejected pending revisions.

30. The PT should update the Proposed System General Flowchart, I80, to reflect the system as depicted by the documentation and to ensure that the objectives of the system are accomplished in the most effective and efficient manner.

31. The SC and UH meet to review the revised Proposed System General Flowchart. The PTH should explain the flowchart in detail to ensure that each has a thorough understanding of the proposed system. The SC and UH either approve or reject the system. If they reject the flowchart, a memorandum should be compiled to reflect the desired changes. This is sent to the PTH by the SC and/or the UH. If the flowchart is approved, a memorandum is also sent to the PTH by the SC.

32. The PT may use the Decision Tables, II410 and II420, as backup and support to, or—in some cases—in lieu of, the Detail System Flowchart, II400.

33. The PT completes the Detail System Flowchart, II400. The Detail System Flowchart is an in-depth description of the proposed system. The flowchart should include the relationships among all other systems, computer processes (on-line and batch), all input and output, and manual off-line activities (DP and user).

34. The SC and UH review the completed Detail System Flowchart, II400, and Decision Tables, II410 and II420, for completeness, efficiency, effectiveness, and clarity. They orally communicate to the PTH any changes that might be required or their acceptance of the flowchart.

35. The PT makes the changes in the Detail System Flowchart, II400, and/or Decision Tables, II410 and II420, agreed upon by the SC, UH, and PTH. The flowchart is then resubmitted to the SC and UH for review.

36. At this point in the system development process, the proposed system is well defined and has been scrutinized by all concerned. The PTH compiles a System Status Report, I140, to be submitted to the ISPC. The report should include a copy of an up-to-date Work Progress Chart, II320. If the project has been delayed and is behind schedule, the PTH should explain, in the SSR, the reasons for the delay. Other information pertinent to project completion, and ultimately to system implementation, should also be included.

37. A copy of the SSR (Work Progress Chart included) should be distributed to each ISPC member at least 1 week prior to the scheduled ISPC meeting. Prior to the meeting, a member may request, from the PTH, further information contained in the system documentation. The PTH, or his or her representative, is obliged to fulfill the request. Any or all of the PT members may be present at the ISPC meeting upon request by the ISPCH.

However, the PTH should be present at the portion of the ISPC meeting in which the SSR is reviewed to ensure that misunderstandings about the system do not occur and to answer any questions that ISPC members might have concerning the system.

The ISPCH submits a memorandum to the PTH expressing the feeling of the ISPC about the progress of the project. The ISPC can express its desires for the revision of resource allocations or general system changes in this memo. If progress is acceptable, the PT should continue progress towards project completion. If changes are required, the PT should make the appropriate changes, or show reasons why these changes should not be made at a subsequent ISPC meeting.

38. The PT makes revisions as required by the ISPC. The PTH completes an SSR, I140, which reflects these changes and submits it to the ISPCH. The ISPCH can elect to accept the changes, or call a general ISPC meeting to review the changes. If the ISPCH accepts the changes, the PT should continue progress towards project completion. If the ISPCH rejects the changes, then he or she should write a memo to the PTH that reflects the reasons for rejecting the SSR. The PTH is obliged to make the required changes and resubmit a subsequent SSR to the ISPCH.

39. Based on file and/or data base size, estimated programming complexity, software requirements, required I/O devices, turnaround and response time requirements, etc., the PT assesses the capability of the present configuration relative to system needs. If the PT determines that more computer hardware is required, then it proceeds with the hardware evaluation and selection process. If the present configuration is acceptable, there is no need to acquire additional capacity.

40. The DPM is responsible for, but not necessarily in charge of, all hardware selection. The hardware selection and evaluation process is detailed, step by step, in Chapter 11. If the proposed acquisition is large enough to merit the formation of an ad hoc hardware selection committee, then the DPM should exercise his/her authority to form the committee. The PTH and/or another member of the PT should be a member of the selection committee. If a committee is formed, then the committee is responsible for all Chapter 11 procedures. The PTH is solely responsible for Chapter 11 procedures when the proposed acquisition is minor and a selection committee is not required.

41. The PT completes the Printer Layouts, II430. The purpose for completing the Printer Layouts is to portray line or character printer-produced outputs in a format that a programmer can use in writing the program(s) necessary to produce the report or document. For those reports and documents that require preprinted forms, a commercial forms representative should be contacted in order to aid in the design of the preprinted forms.

Also, the PT completes the CRT Layouts, II440. The purpose for completing the CRT Layout is to portray a CRT display in a format that a programmer can use in writing the program(s) necessary to produce the display.

42. The PT is responsible for design of and information included on all manually produced reports and documents that originate within the scope of the system. The PT may revise, initiate, or delete any report or document in the system depending upon what is required to meet the objectives of the proposed system; however, any change should be coordinated with the primary and secondary users to ensure completeness and usability. Any changes of status of an existing report or document, or addition or deletion of a report or document, should be reflected by updating the System Reports and Documents, I40.

Note: This block activity includes all formatted logs used for system control, either user or DP.

43. The SC and UH review the Printer and CRT Layouts, II430 and II440, and the layouts of the manually produced reports and documents. The PTH should be present at the meeting to answer any questions about the documentation. The SC and UH orally communicate any required changes to any or all of the above. The PTH should make notes of the required changes. If no changes are necessary, the PT continues work towards project completion.

44. The PT makes the necessary revisions to the layouts. A full review of the revisions is not necessary. The SC and UH are each asked to review that portion of the documentation on which he or she requested a change. After all changes are made and have passed the scrutiny of the SC and/or UH as appropriate, the PT continues towards project completion.

45. The PT completes the Keypunch Descriptions, II450, and Key-to-Disk Descriptions, II460. The purpose of these reports is to set forth the instructions for data entry personnel.

46. The PT reviews and revises the Cost Report, I120. Based on more recent and accurate information about the proposed system (hardware, scope, personnel, etc.), the cost estimates of Phase I should be updated if necessary.

In addition to updating the Cost Report, the PTH should prepare an itemized summary of the differences that exist between the initial Cost

Report and the revised Cost Report. The Summary should be in the form of a memorandum and should be submitted to the ISPCH for review. The memo should contain the percentage increase or decrease in the total estimated system development costs (Phases I and II) and the percentage increase or decrease in the total estimated monthly recurring costs after system implementation. Other pertinent information should be included at the discretion of the PTH.

47. If a cost overrun of greater than 12% (arbitrary, depending on corporate policy) exists for either the developmental costs or the recurring costs or both, the revised Cost Report should be reviewed by the ISPC. A 12% buffer for estimation error should be implied in the ISPC acceptance of a proposed system. However, an error of greater than 12% may require major revisions in the proposed system and/or funding source(s). In that case, a formal meeting of the ISPC should be called to act on the cost overrun.

48. The ISPC meets to discuss the severity of the cost overrun and possible alternative actions. The ISPC can elect to table the project, request revisions be made that might affect the system cost, or approve the system with the overrun. The ISPCH should write a memorandum to be distributed to the PTH, UH, and DPM that reflects the outcome of the meeting.

49. The ISPCH completes the SSR, I140, that reflects the decision to terminate work on the proposed system. Appropriate comments should be included to relate the reasons for project termination and other pertinent information, as required. The SSR should be distributed to the PTH, UH, the DPM.

50. The PT is responsible for assessing the feasibility of reducing the scope of the system to meet budgetary limitations. If the PT determines that limiting the scope of the system would be inconsistent with project objectives, the PTH writes a memo to the ISPCH that reflects its assessment. If a system revision is deemed feasible, then the PT begins work on the necessary revision.

51. The ISPC reconsiders the cost overrun in light of the PT assessment that the system cannot adequately be modified so that project cost remains within the budgetary limitations. The ISPC can either approve continuation of the project with a cost overrun or terminate the project.

52. Same as Block 49.

53. If the ISPC approves project continuation with a cost overrun, the responsibility for allocating the overrun costs to the various budget units rests with the ISPC. The ISPCH and the ISPC liaison serve as chief negotiators. After having identified the source(s) of additional project funds, the ISPCH should prepare an SSR, I140, that details the funding source(s). A copy is then sent to the head of each budget center affected.

54. The PT describes, in general, the revisions necessary to bring the project cost in line with allocated funds. The revisions should be written in paragraph format and included in a memo to the ISPC. The revisions should be discussed in sufficient detail to serve as a guide for the PT through the revision process and to allow the PT to make reasonable estimates of the revised costs. The ramifications of all new trade-offs should be addressed in the discussions (e.g., response time increase from 3 to 15 seconds, daily versus weekly reports, on-line CRT's versus COM, etc.).

55. The PT revises Cost Report, I120, to reflect the system revisions.

56. The ISPC meets to evaluate the proposed revisions and the revised Cost Report. The ISPC can either request additional revisions, terminate the project, or approve the revised system as presented. The PTH should be present at the ISPC meeting to answer questions about the revised system. If the ISPC requests that additional revisions be made, these should be detailed in a memorandum to the PTH. If the revisions and Cost Report are approved, the ISPCH should send a memo to the PTH reflecting the approval.

57. The PT modifies the original revisions description memo to accommodate any subsequent revisions requested by the ISPC.

58. Same as Block 49.

59. The PT modifies all existing system documentation to accommodate the approved revised system description. A change to any existing documentation should be reviewed by the same person(s) who originally approved the documentation. These reviews should be scheduled, as required, and on an informal basis. At the discretion of the PTH, any or all of the procedures set forth in the Work Flow Diagrams and/or Block Descriptions may be used depending upon the extent of the required revisions.

60. The PTH calls a meeting of the DPM, SC, and UH to review all revisions made to the proposed system. The PTH, and other PT members, as needed, should present an oral summary of the revisions. The DPM, SC, and UH either reject or approve the documentation revisions as presented. If the revisions are rejected, the SC should orally communicate the required changes to the PTH.

61. The PT makes the revisions to the system documentation as requested by the DPM, SC, and UH. Depending upon the extent of the changes made, the PTH can elect either to call a review meeting of the DPM, SC, and UH or to contact each individually and conduct the review informally.

62. The PTH should contact at least one computer-forms representative and assign a team member to work with him or her in the design of all preprinted forms. Depending on the required order lead time, the PTH may elect to recommend ordering all or part of the forms now or to wait until a later date. A copy of each preprinted form should be appended to the appropriate report or document in the System Reports and Documents, I40.

63. The SC appoints specific programmers to the PT according to the specifications set forth in the Estimated Personnel Requirements, II300. Note that all or part of the required programmers may have been appointed earlier in Phase II, Part 1. If this is the case, the SC need only appoint the programmer(s) necessary to fulfill the predetermined PT complement of programmers.

64. The PT completes the Program Descriptions, II490. The PT should examine the Detail System Flowchart, II400, in order to identify and define the programs and program modules that are required for the most effective and efficient system.

65. The SC reviews all of the Program Descriptions for completeness, clarity, and uniformity. The Program Descriptions are not necessarily completed by the individual who ultimately writes the program; therefore, the descriptions should be comprehensive enough so a programmer who is unfamiliar with the system could write a required program having only the Program Description and associated system documentation with no additional verbal or written explanations. If this is not the case, the SC should reject the Program Description and communicate to the PTH any deficiencies in it. The SC should evaluate the Program Descriptions individually.

66. The members of the PT that compiled a specific rejected Program Description make the required revisions. The revised Program Descriptions are then resubmitted to the SC for review.

67. The SC reviews all existing system documentation for neatness and uniformity. At this point in Phase II, all of the system documentation has been reviewed in detail at least once. The purpose of the examination by the SC is to ensure that general guidelines have been followed during preparation, that the documentation is legible with good readability, and that it is uniform throughout.

After having reviewed the documentation the SC calls a meeting with the PT to discuss any required revisions to the documentation. All required revisions are verbally communicated to the PT at this time by the SC.

68. The PT makes the revisions to the system documentation as required.

69. The PTH calls a meeting with the DPM, SC, and UH to evaluate the project progress and to assess the need to revise the Work Progress Chart, II320. As a rule of thumb, the target dates on the Work Progress Chart should be revised if the work on the project is either ahead of or behind schedule by 20% of the estimated total time for Phase II. That is, if Phase II is estimated to be 100 days in duration and the Work Progress Chart reflects 25 days behind, then work is 25% behind schedule and consideration should be given to revising the Work Progress Chart in order to more accurately reflect project progress.

70. The DPM, SC, UH, and PTH revise the Work Progress Chart, II320, to reflect more realistic target dates for the remainder of Phase II.

71. The PTH completes a System Status Report, I140, that reflects the completion of Phase II, Part 1 and the general progress of the project. The SSR and the original (if applicable) and revised (if applicable) Work Progress Charts are sent to the ISPCH.

Documentation Instructions and Forms—Phase II, Part 1

ESTIMATED PERSONNEL REQUIREMENTS—II300

Instructions

Form: II300.

Responsibility: Project Team Head (PTH).

Content: The projected personnel requirements for Phase II are listed for the Computer Center and each user department and/or division involved in the system development process. The project team (PT) members should be included.

Include the following information for each individual:

1. Department/division affiliation. List those with the same affiliation together.
2. Functional title of individual. Use corporate classification only if representative of function (e.g., list Systems Coordinator instead of Systems Analyst II).
3. Percentage of total working time (40 hours/week) required throughout Part 1 of Phase II.
4. Percentage of total working time required throughout Part 2 of Phase II.
5. Percentage of total working time required throughout Part 3 of Phase II.

When approved by all managers concerned, this report serves to document the personnel commitments required for system development. This report can be updated as required but only with the consent of the managers involved. The report should be updated as required to reflect the actual personnel requirements.

REPORT TITLE ESTIMATED PERSONNEL REQUIREMENTS	NO. II300	DATE
SYSTEM TITLE		ID

DEPARTMENT/DIVISION	FUNCTIONAL TITLE	PHASE II – % TIME PART 1	PART 2	PART 3
(1)	(2)	(3)	(4)	(5)

PERSONNEL TRAINING REQUIREMENTS—II310

Instructions

Form: General Purpose, G10.

Responsibility: Project Team Head.

Content: The purpose of the Personnel Training Requirements report is to document training required for individuals and groups that will be involved in the system development process and system operation (user, DP, ISPC, etc.).

List the names (if known) and titles of the individuals who will require some type of training. Groups of persons requiring similar training may be listed together (e.g., key-to-disk operators). Include the following for each individual or group requiring training:

1. Training required. Brief description of type of training.
2. Where training will be conducted and by whom (e.g., in-house by systems analysts; IBM Education Center in Chicago, etc.).
3. Time frame. Time period during which the training will be conducted relative to the Work Flow Diagrams. For example, "the training will be conducted starting 2 weeks prior to the estimated start of Block 30, Phase II, Part 1, and continue for 5 days."

The above three items should be included for each category of training administered to each person or group.

WORK PROGRESS CHART—II320

Instructions

Form: II320.

Responsibility: Project Team Head.

Content: The Work Progress Chart is used in conjunction with the Work Flow Diagrams of Phase II for the purpose of illustrating the estimated time schedule and the actual progress towards completion of the estimated time schedule. The Work Progress Chart is a project management tool.

The Work Progress Chart has two parts. The first part is simply a tally of completed reports for Phases I and II. The reports are checked off as they are completed. Note that Phase I reports may require updating during Phase II and should not be checked off until each has been reviewed and approved initially in Phase II. Each Phase II report is checked off after the initial review and acceptance, even though the report may require updating throughout Phase II. This continuous tally provides an individual with the means for determining the availability of any given report and the overall status of report preparation.

The second part of the Work Progress Chart is the means for estimating the work schedule and monitoring the progress of a project. Included in this part are numbers that correspond to the blocks of Phase II, Parts 1, 2, and 3. The PT estimates the date (month/day/year) on which it will begin an activity of a certain block on the Work Flow Diagrams. It needs only to estimate those dates for blocks that have boxes above and below the block number. These dates are milestones during Phase II. A record is also kept of actual dates and, therefore, the days ahead or behind schedule. Also, a record is kept of those blocks completed or not applicable.

The following entries should be made in pencil continually throughout Phase II:

1. Three marks can be made in the boxes which correspond to the various reports. As preparation is begun on any report, a diagonal (/) is placed in the box corresponding to the report. Place an "X" in the box once the report has been reviewed and approved initially. Many reports, such as the Record Layout, II380, may require separate reports for as many records as required. In such cases place the total number of that particular report just below the appropriate box. Mark "X" only when all are complete. Depending on the scope of the proposed system, certain reports may not be required. In such cases place an "O" in the appropriate box.

2. Three marks can be made in the numbered boxes. As each block activity is begun, a diagonal (/) is placed in the numbered box corresponding to the numbered block in the Work Flow Diagrams. After the activity has been completed, the box should be filled with an "X." Depending on the decision alternative at a given block, certain block activities may or may not be required. As it becomes apparent that an activity is not required, that block number should be circled (e.g., "O").

Note: Although numerical sequencing of the DP Manual is basically sound, circumstance may dictate that certain activities be started and/or completed out of sequence. Also note that many of the activities are to be started at the same time (parallel activities). These activities are bracketed below the activity boxes.

3. The month and year (e.g., June '79) that correspond to the estimated start date (see number 4 below) of that block activity.
4. Day of the month that work is expected to begin on the block activity indicated.
5. The month and year that correspond to the actual start date (see number 6 below) that the block activity was begun. Omit this entry if the estimated and actual start dates are within the same month.
6. Day of the month that work actually began on the block activity indicated.
7. Determine the number of working days (based on 5 days/week) difference between the estimated and actual start dates. Indicate status by placing the number of days ahead or behind in the appropriate box. Use "A" for ahead and "B" for behind (e.g., 5 days behind would be "5B").

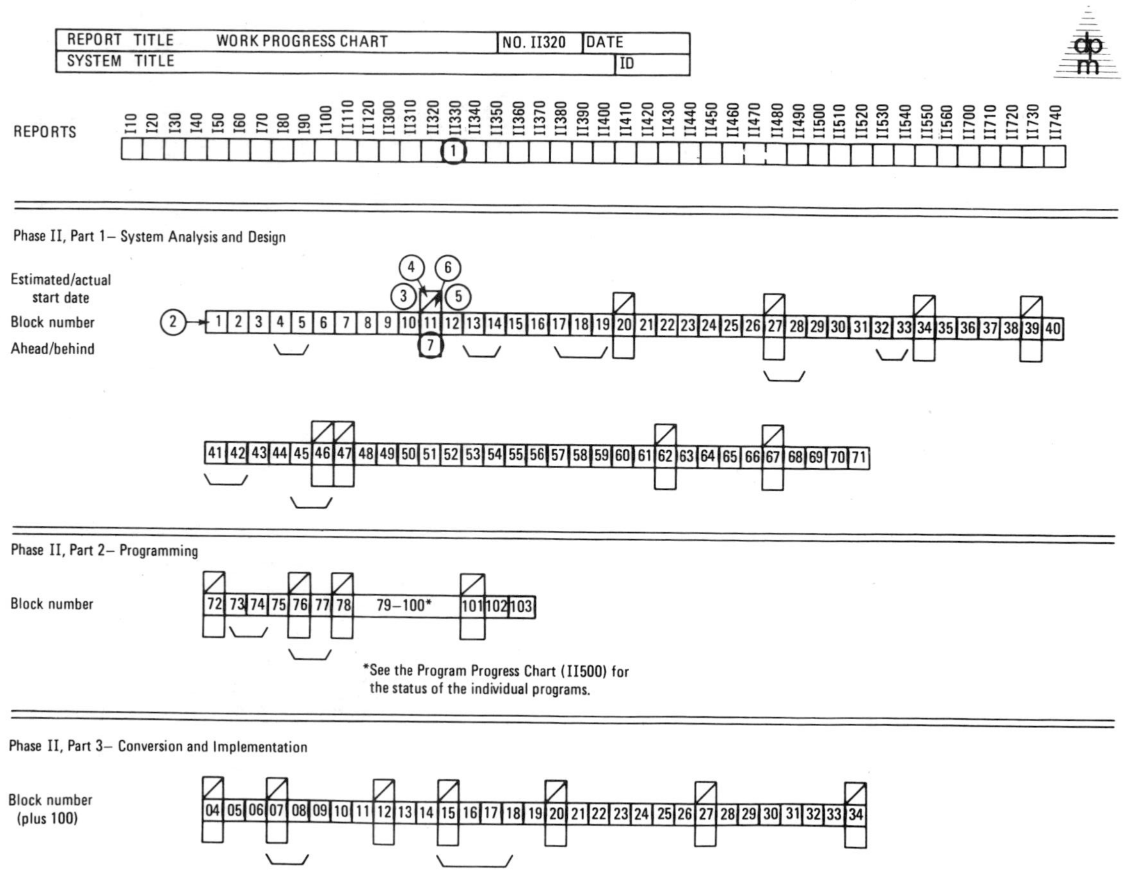

(actual size is 11" × 16")

OUTPUT DESCRIPTION—II340

Instructions

Form: II330.

Responsibility: Project Team Head.

Content: The Output Reference List is a list of all output of reports, displays, or transaction documents that have an output medium of punched cards, line or character printer, or CRT. Each output is given a title and a number (for control purposes). Each entry on the list will ultimately have associated with it an Output Description, II340, and an output layout, II380 for cards, II430 for printer, and II440 for CRT. The Output Reference List is a cover for the Output Descriptions and layouts.

The following information should be included for each report, display, or transaction document:

1. Title. Title should be brief (no more than 40 characters) but descriptive.
2. Output identification (ID). The ID consists of eight alphanumeric characters used to designate the program, system, and output. The first four numeric characters designate the program which is used to produce the output. The next two alpha characters designate the system and should be descriptive (e.g., PR for payroll). The last two numeric characters designate the output number for a given program. For example, a "0001PR01" designates output number one of payroll program one. (Note that the program ID is six characters and does not include the last two digits.) The output ID is entered by the programmer during Phase II, Part 2.
3. Medium. Type of device used for producing the output.
4. Description complete. Once the Output Description, II340, has been completed, enter the number of the II340 that corresponds to the report.
5. Layout complete. Once the layout—II380, II430, or II440—has been completed, enter the number of the layout form (should correspond to II340 number). See "Note" at the end of the II380 instructions.
6. Total number of pages of the Output Reference List.
7. Page number.

The Output Descriptions and layouts are filed with the reference list in numeric order as they are completed.

REPORT TITLE OUTPUT REFERENCE LIST	NO. II330	DATE
SYSTEM TITLE		ID

TITLE	ID	MEDIUM	DESCRIPTION NO.	LAYOUT NO.
(1)	(2)	(3)	(4)	(5)

Page (7)/(6)

OUTPUT DESCRIPTION—II340

Instructions

Form: II340.

Responsibility: Project Team Head.

Content: The purpose of the Output Description is to describe each computer-produced system output that is either a report, display, or transaction.

The output medium can be punched card, line or character printer, or CRT. Information included on the Output Description should include:

1. Title. As described in II330.
2. ID. As described in II330.
3. Cycle. Preparation cycle, e.g., daily, weekly, etc.
4. Primary user, The department and/or division controlling the use of the output.
5. Type of input. Place an "X" in the appropriate box for either printer, card, or CRT.
6. Number of copies printed. If printer not used, put "NA."
7. Burst. Put either "yes," "no," or "NA."
8. Decollate. Put either "yes," "no," or "NA." Place an asterisk by "yes" if it is necessary to subdivide the report, and indicate full instructions for subdividing and routing in the purpose and description section, item 11.
9. Interpret. Either "yes" or "no." (Reference appropriate card layout for interpret instructions.)
10. Hard copy option. Either "yes" or "no" depending on whether a user requires a hard copy of a particular CRT display.
11. Describe the purpose of the report or document and explain its use for each department or division using this output. Other pertinent information should be included in this section as required.
12. Copy numbers. Put copy number or numbers to be distributed to indicated department or division (e.g., 1,6). "NA" for all but printer output.
13. Department/division. Department and/or division of the user. List all users of the output.

14. Location. Building and room number and/or address, if required.

15. A unique number that corresponds to the number on the associated layout forms, II380, II430, and II440.

REPORT TITLE OUTPUT DESCRIPTION	NO. II340	DATE
SYSTEM TITLE		ID

Title ______ (1) ______ ID ______ (2) ______

Cycle ______ (3) ______ Primary User ______ (4) ______

(5) Printer- No. of Copies ______ (6) ______ Burst ______ (7) ______ Decollate ______ (8) ______

☐ Card— Interpret ______ (9) ______

☐ CRT— Hard Copy Option ______ (10) ______

Purpose and Description

(11)

Copy Nos.	Department/Division	Location
(12)	(13)	(14)

Number (15)

DATA ELEMENT MATRIX—II350

Instructions

Form: II350.

Responsibility: Project Team Head.

Content: The purpose of the Data Element Matrix is to list all data elements that are part of the system. These may be extracted from source documents, generated by the system, or constants used in the system. The matrix should be updated as required and should serve as a guide for uniformity in data element use throughout Phase II.

1. Data element number. An arbitrary reference number which is helpful for cross-reference when supplemental forms are required for expanding the number of source documents, reports, files, and data base records that can be referenced. Enter this number diagonally across the box.

2. A brief descriptive title for the data element (e.g., Employee ID).

3. Data label. The label used in programs to reference the data element (to be supplied by programmers during Phase II, Part 2). Use rules, applicable to the programming language used, for characters and length.

4. Number of positions. Indicate the number of bytes of secondary storage required for this element.

5. Picture/format. For business-oriented programming language interfaces, use the standard S, V, X, and 9 picture characters to indicate the file storage format [e.g., 9(5)V9(2), XXX]. For scientific programming language interfaces, use the standard I, F, E, and A formats to indicate the file storage format.

Note: If the data element is a single of multidimensional array, note the dimensions beside the "picture/format" [e.g., 99V99(20)—occurs 20 times or I5 (50, 10) $-$ 50 $\times$ 10 integer array].

6. Storage. For business languages indicate storage as follows:

E—EBCDIC
P—packed decimal
B—binary
F—floating point

For scientific languages indicate precision as follows:

leave blank—single precision

D—double precision

7. Description. Use this space for an expanded description of the data element if necessary (note that some titles are self-explanatory and further description is not required). Descriptions that require more space should be included in the Glossary, I100, under the data element's title, in which case, put "see Glossary" under the descriptions.
8. Coded. Indicate if data element is coded by placing the page number of the appropriate Data Element Codes, II360; otherwise, leave blank.
9. Responsibility. Define work center responsible for update of the data element.
10. Source document, report, file, or data base. The full or abbreviated titles of source documents, reports, files, or data base records on which the listed data elements appear. Group each category (e.g., all files listed together, etc.). Preceding each name place "S" for source document, "R" for report (or for a transaction document, e.g., paycheck or CRT display), "F" for file, and "D" for a data base record.

Note: Find the source document and report titles on System Reports and Documents, I40, and the file and data base record titles on Data Base/File Descriptions, II370.

11. Data occurrence. Indicate each occurrence of a given data element in a source document, report, or file by placing an "X" in the appropriate column. If the occurrence of the element is variable, indicate by placing a "V" instead of an "X."
12. Total number of pages of II350 required to describe all of the system data elements. Include only pages that have a unique set of data elements.
13. Page number for the Data Element Matrix. Note that in some cases more souce documents, reports, and files may exist than there are columns on a single copy of Form II350. In order to be comprehensive, include a second page that has only the corresponding data element number and the remaining source document names, etc. Number the first page "1a," the second "1b," and so on.

REPORT TITLE DATA ELEMENT MATRIX	NO. II350	DATE
SYSTEM TITLE		ID

No.	TITLE		DESCRIPTION			CODED	SOURCE DOCUMENTS (S), REPORT (R), FILE (F), or DATA BASE (D)
	LABEL	NO. POS.	PICTURE/FORMAT	STORAGE	RESPONSIBILITY		(10)
(1)		(2)		(7)		(8)	(11)
	(3)	(4)	(5)	(6)	(9)		

(actual size is 11" × 16")

Page (13) / (12)

DATA ELEMENT CODES—II360

Instructions

Form: II360.

Responsibility: Project Team Head.

Content: A Data Element Codes form should be completed for each data element that has a coding scheme. The purpose of this form is to detail this coding scheme.

1. Data element title. As listed on the Data Element Matrix, II350.
2. Label. As listed on Data Element Matrix.
3. Number of positions. As listed on Data Element Matrix.
4. Positions. This column contains the position number(s) of a particular code within the data element (numbered left to right). List all position numbers which apply for one level of the code. For example, a six-digit employee number might designate department first two positions), division (third digit), and unique employee (fourth-sixth positions). The "positions" column would contain "1,2" as a first entry. The second entry would be "3" and located on the line following the last "code" entry (see number 6 below) for department. The last entry in this column would be "4,5,6" and located on the line following the last "code" entry for division.
5. Alpha and/or numeric. For positions indicated put "A," "N," and "A/N."
6. Code. List in alphabetic and/or numeric order the actual codes for the positions indicated.
7. Description. Description of associated code value.

Note: The following example illustrates for the above-coded employee number how entries 4, 5, 6, and 7 would be listed.

1, 2	N	10	Accounting
		11	Financial planning
		20	Engineering
		21	Production control
		25	Personnel
3	N	1	San Francisco
		2	New York

4, 5, 6	N	—	Unique 3-digit employee number within department within division. Assigned by personnel office.

8. Comment. Other pertinent information regarding the coded data element.
9. Total number of coded data elements.
10. Each coded data element has a unique page number (1, 2, 3, etc.). If the coded values are extensive and require additional Form II360's for a given data element, number the first "1a," the second "1b," and so on.

REPORT TITLE DATA ELEMENT CODES	NO. II360	DATE
SYSTEM TITLE		ID

Data Element Title: (1)	
Label: (2)	No. of Positions: (3)

POSITION	A/N	CODE	DESCRIPTION
(4)	(5)	(6)	(7)

Comments: (8) ____________________

____

____

PAGE (10)/(9)

DATA BASE/FILE DESCRIPTION—II370

Instructions

Forms: II370; General Purpose, G10.

Responsibility: Project Team Head.

> *Note:* If a data base administrator exists within the Computer Center and is not on the project team, the PTH should cooperate with the data base administrator in the completion of II370 and II390.

Content: The purpose of II370 is twofold. It is the primary document used to describe the traditional files, either computer or manual, and/or data bases for the proposed system. For clarity the instructions are presented separately but the same form is used.

File Description

Content: The purpose of the File Description is to define the type and use of a file and to list the data elements associated with the file. A completed II370 report and the Record Layout, II380, constitute the documentation for a file. The files are described by logical records and the data elements within those records. This report supersedes the System Data Files, I50, of Phase I. Put "NA" in all blanks that are not applicable to the named file.

1. Title of the file.
2. Record title.
3. Storage medium. Indicate type of storage medium such as punch card, tape, disk, etc.
4. File label. The file label used by programs for referencing the file.
5. Approximate number of records. This figure is intended to give persons concerned an idea of the approximate size of the file.
6. Variable or fixed-length records. Put "V" or "F" as applicable.
7. Number of alphanumeric characters contained in a logical record. If variable, put the minimum and maximum possible (e.g., 102–214).
8. Number of bytes contained in a logical record. If variable, put the minimum and maximum possible (e.g., 85–170).
9. Encoding system. Indicate encoding system used for character representation. If more than one is used, indicate each with the most used first (e.g., EBCDIC, packed decimal).

10. Record sequence. If records are arranged within the file in a specific sequence, list the title(s) of the control data element(s) that govern the sequencing. If more than one field governs the sequence, list in major to minor order. Indicate whether sequence is ascending or descending.

Numbers 11, 12, 13, 14, and 15 are applicable for magnetic tape files only.

11. Density. BPI.

12. Number of tracks.

13. Blocking factor. Indicate number of logical records/block. Put "std" for system-supplied blocking.

14. External label and volume number. The external label should be the same as the file label used in programs, if possible. If file label is not sufficient to identify the file, expand the external label as required. For multivolume files append a "−1," "−2," and so on to the label to distinguish between volumes. Include the volume number(s) in this space also.

15. Other pertinent descriptive information regarding the tape file.

Numbers 16, 17, 18, 19, and 20 are applicable for disk files only.

16. Type of file organization (sequential, random, index-sequential).

17. External label and volume number. The external label should be the same as the file label used in programs. For multivolume files, append a "-1," "-2," and so on to the label to distinguish between the disk packs.

18. File location. Indicate volume number(s) and the associated cylinders used for storage of the file.

19. Index location. Indicate volume number(s) and the associated cylinders used for storage of the index.

20. Other pertinent descriptive information regarding the disk file.

21. Data element number. Number each data element in ascending order according to the position of appearance in the record. Note that II370, part 2, can be used to extend the data element list if more space is required.

22. Data element title. Same as on Data Element Matrix, II350.

23. Data element label. Same as on Data Element Matrix, II350.

24. Date Element Matrix number. The number which corresponds to the data element in the Data Element Matrix, II350.

25. Comments. Comments pertinent to a full description of the data element. Bracket data elements within a repeating group and indicate the maximum number possible.

26. Total number of files within the system.

27. Each file has a unique page number (1, 2, 3, etc.). Number in this space all pages associated with a given file (supplemental data element lists, general file description, G10, etc., with a unique number and an alphabetic letter—first "1a," second "1b," and so on).

28. General description of the file. Use the General Purpose Form, G10, to describe the use of the file in paragraph format. Include such information as other system interfaces, frequency of use, backup requirements, volatility of records or of particular data elements, and other information required for a complete description of the file.

Data Base Description

Content: The purpose of the Data Base Description is to identify all records (segments) in the data base and all data elements in each record. A completed II370 and the Data Base Schema, II390, constitute the documentation for a data base. Put "NA" in all blanks which are not applicable to the named data base.

1. Title of the data base.

2. Not applicable.

3. Storage medium. Indicate type of random access storage medium.

4, 5, 6, 7, 8, 9. Same as "File" instructions.

10, 11, 12, 13, 14, 15. Not applicable.

16. Organization. Indicate name of data base management system used.

17, 18, 19, 20. Same as "File" instructions.

21, 22, 23, 24, 25. As a data base may have numerous records, the data elements are listed for each record according to the position of appearance in the record. This section will contain a listing of all records in the data base; therefore, for a given data base, only one II370 is completed.

21. Data element number. Place an "X" here to indicate the beginning of a particular record. Subsequent to the "X," number each data element in ascending order according to its position of appearance in the record. Use as many II370, part 2's as needed to detail all records. Always skip two lines between records.

22. Data element/record title. Use this space when adjacent to an "X" in the "No." column to include the title of a record. Subsequent to the record title, list the title of all data elements within that record. The data element titles should be the same as the titles on the Data Element Matrix, II350.

23, 24, 25. Same as "File" instructions.

26. Total number of pages, parts 1 and 2, required to list all records of the data base.

27. Page number of data base description package.

REPORT TITLE DATA BASE/FILE DESCRIPTION (part 1)	NO. II370	DATE
SYSTEM TITLE		ID

Data Base/File Title ______ (1) ______ Record Title ______ (2) ______

Medium ______ (3) ______ Label ______ (4) ______ Approx. No. Records ______ (5) ______

Record Length: V/F ______ (6) ______ Characters ______ (7) ______ Bytes ______ (8) ______ Encoding System ______ (9) ______

Record Sequence ______ (10) ______

For Magnetic Tape: Density ______ (11) ______ Tracks ______ (12) ______ Blocking Factor ______ (13) ______

External Label and Vol. No. ______ (14) ______

Other ______ (15) ______

For Disk: Organization ______ (16) ______

External Label and Vol. No. ______ (17) ______

File Location ______ (18) ______

Index Location ______ (19) ______

Other ______ (20) ______

DATA ELEMENTS OF LOGICAL RECORD

No.	Title	Label	Matrix No.	Comments
(21)	(22)	(23)	(24)	(25)

PAGE (27) / (26)

REPORT TITLE DATA BASE/FILE DESCRIPTION (part 2)	No. II370	DATE
SYSTEM TITLE		ID

DATA ELEMENTS (continued)

No.	Title	Label	Matrix No.	Comments
(21)	(22)	(23)	(24)	(25)

Page (27) / (26)

RECORD LAYOUT—II380

Instructions

Form: II380.

Responsibility: Project Team Head.

Content: The Record Layout is general and can be used to depict the record layout for all files recorded on a machine-readable medium (card, tape, disk, etc.). The Record Layout graphically illustrates the relationship between the fields, the field formats and the field lengths.

The grid of II380 is set up to depict a record up to 600 bytes and/or characters. Should there be a need to depict a record of greater length, simply continue the record on another Form II380. There are six rows of 100 positions numbered at the top of the form. Record layouts for cards should have one block corresponding to one column. Record layouts for primary and secondary storage should have one block corresponding to one byte. Below the blocks is space for other pertinent field information.

1. Title of the file.

2. Record title.

3. Storage medium. Indicate type of storage medium such as punch card, tape, disk, etc.

4. File label. The file label used by programs for referencing the file.

5. If the storage medium is punched card, scratch out the hundreds (100, 200, etc.) numbers on the left side of the form, and put "card no. 1." If more than one card is required for the record, put "card no. 2" on the second row. Use only the first 80 (or 96, as applicable) columns for card records.

   If the record length exceeds 600 characters, place the appropriate hundreds number (600, 700, 800, etc.) on the left side of the form.

6. This space can be used for several purposes. The length of the field should be noted by a vertical line drawn at the end of each field. If this space permits, place here the data element title or label (if descriptive). If this is not possible (e.g., 1, 2, or 3 position field) enter the appropriate data element number found on the File Description, II370 (NOT Data Element Matrix number).

   This space can also be used to indicate the decimal format of a numeric value. Use the designator "L.R" to indicate the number of positions to the left "L," and the right "R" of the decimal (e.g., "6.2" means 6 to the left, and 2 to the right). If the field is packed, place "P" after the "L.R" (e.g., 6.2P).

Note: If space permits, the option exists to include the data element picture from the Data Element Matrix, II350.

Indicate repeated groups and/or data elements with a solid horizontal line drawn 1/8 inch below the numbered blocks. The line should cover all data elements in the repeated group. Above the line, write the name of the repeated group and indicate, in parentheses, the maximum number of times the group can be repeated [e.g., "statement" line entry (20)].

For each group (data aggregate, record, segment in DBMS's), indicate the primary key by underlining the data element title or label. When the primary key is concatenated, the data elements of the key should be adjacent to one another if possible. All primary keys of a group are underlined, and a curved line over the record strip should be drawn to connect the data elements of the concatenated key.

Note that secondary keys within a record are noted by enclosing the key name in parentheses [e.g., "(Date)"].

7. Format. Place the coded letter describing the block format in each block—"A" for alphabetic, "N" for decimal, "X" for alphanumeric, "B" for binary, and "P" for packed decimal. For example, enter "NNNNN"for a five-digit employee number.
8. Total number of record layouts for machine-readable files in the system. This number should be the same as the total number of files from the File Description, II370.
9. Each record layout has a unique page number which should be the same as that of the associated file. Should the record length exceed the capacity of a single record layout form (600 bytes), then the supplemental forms for the same record should be numbered "1a," "1b," and so on.

Note: The Record Layout form is primarily used to depict file record layouts; however, it is also used for layouts of punched card output. In these cases, with pen and ink, change items 1, 2, and 4 to "output title," "output ID," and "output description number," respectively. Do not include punched card output layouts in the total number of Record Layouts in item 8, and ignore item 9.

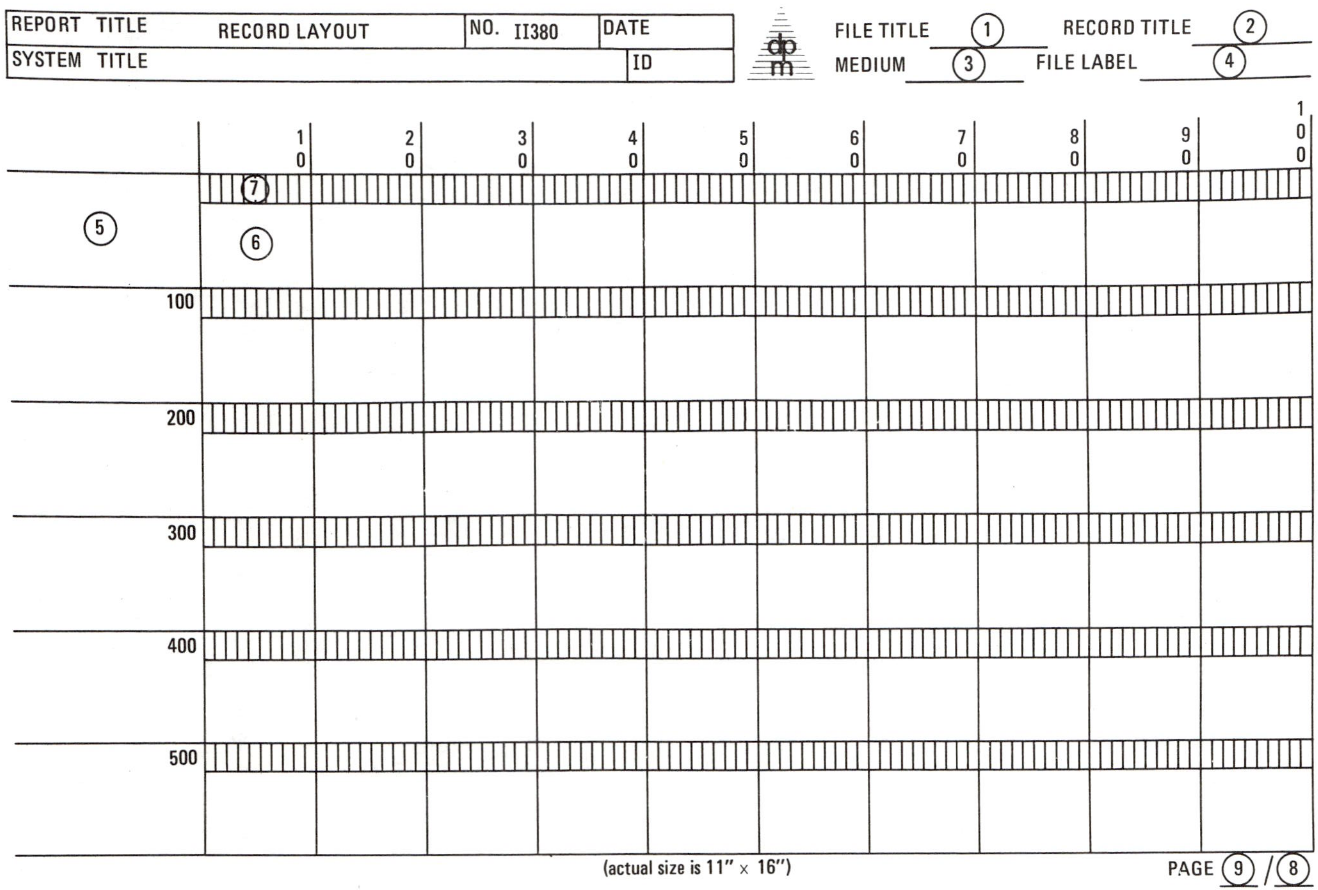

(actual size is 11" × 16")

DATA BASE SCHEMA—II390

Instructions

Form: General Purpose, G10 (11 × 16 inches).

Note: Complex schemas may require a larger presentation area.

Responsibility: Project Team Head.

Note: See II370 "Responsibility."

Content: The purpose of the Data Base Schema is to provide a graphical representation of the logical structure of the data base. The schema can be used to represent the data elements, data aggregates and records (and/or IBM segments), and their logical relationships to each other. Also, the schema can be used to indicate the CODASYL sets and areas. The schema is not applicable to computer centers that do not have data base management software or systems.

Because of the widespread use of alternative data base nomenclature among computer hardware and software vendors, the following definitions are suggested for use in the DP Manual.

Data Element. The smallest logical unit of data (e.g., zip code).

Data Aggregate. A logically related collection of data elements within a record. A data aggregate is primarily used to identify an "aggregate" of data elements (or a single data element) that are or that can be repeated within a record (e.g., the students' names and ID's on a particular course record).

Note: Data aggregates usually have a limited number of occurrences.

Record. A group of related data elements and/or data aggregates that are usually retrieved as a unit by the applications program.

Set. A set can be described on the schema for each "one to many" record relationship. For each owner a set can have an arbitrary number of members.

Singular Set. A singular set is used to provide a simple traditional file within the data base. The singular set has no members but is a system within itself.

Area. A subdivision of addressable secondary storage space, which may contain a record, records, sets, or parts of sets.

The following procedures should be used in graphically depicting the Data Base Schema.

1. Refer to the Data Base Description, II370, in order to identify all data aggregates and records (and/or segments). These will be collectively called "groups" in the following instructions.

2. Use the Record Layout, II380, as an aid to graphically displaying the schema.

First, lay out each group on a separate Form II380, following the instructions set forth in II380. Use as many consecutive "record strips" (II380, items 6 and 7) as required for a given group, then begin a new II380 for each subsequent group.

Second, cut out the completed record strip(s) as one piece for each group. Cut just above the column numbers and on the bottom line of the last filled or partially filled record strip. Cut out the unfilled portion of the last record strip leaving only the detailed data on the group.

Note: Additions to or deletions from the groups can be reflected by reaccomplishing the record strip or by simply physically appending additional data elements, if applicable.

3. Determine the association between appropriate data elements.

The associations within a particular group are implied. That is, all data elements in a group that are not designated as keys (underlined) are attributes of the key(s). These associations are indicated by the record strips.

4. The association between keys is explicit and is indicated by solid lines connecting the appropriate keys. To do this place all key titles that represent groups on a large piece of paper in a circular manner so that a line drawn between any two will not overrun a key title. This provides a worksheet from which the associations can be established and it provides the best approach to the graphic presentation of the schema.

The schema designer can use this worksheet as an aid to grouping sets and/or areas in a manner that will provide clear schema presentation for the applications programmers and analysts.

5. Connect those keys which have an association (relationship) with a solid line, which is always drawn vertically and/or horizontally. The relationships can have several characteristics that can easily be illustrated graphically.

First, establish whether the path between two data elements is one-way or two-way. If the data base logical design requires a path from Key-A to Key-B but not from Key-B to Key-A, the path is one-way and will have an arrow adjacent to and pointing to Key-B only. If a path is also required from Key-B to Key-A, the path is two-way, and each end of the connecting line will have an arrow adjacent to and pointing to the respective keys.

A link between any two keys will terminate at each end in one of three ways:

a. No arrows

b. One arrow

c. Two arrows

Therefore, the possible key-to-key relationships are as follows:

One-way

——→	one-to-one
——→→	one-to-many

Two-way

←——→	one-to-one
←——→→	one-to-many
←←——→→	many-to-many

6. The graphic technique used to illustrate a named set requires that the association line (between owner/member keys) be broken and the set name be inserted. When this is not possible, write the set name near the association line. To avoid confusion, terminate all named sets by the word "SET." For example,

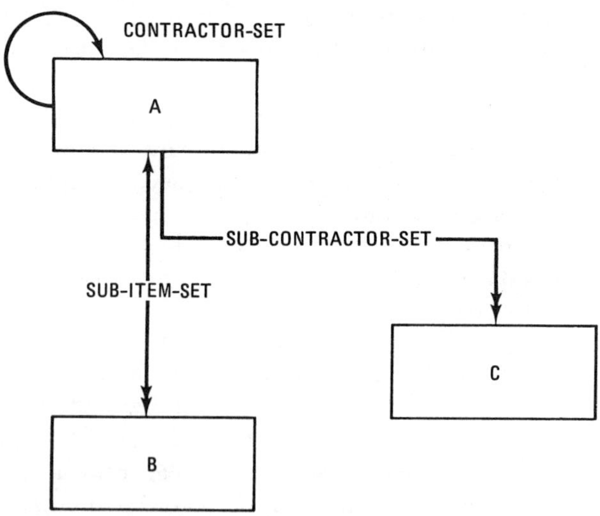

To illustrate a singular set, draw a 270° arc about the key and terminate it with an arrow as shown above for Key-A.

7. Cross-references between like data elements within groups can be noted by a dotted line. The cross-reference lines are merely a convenience and are, therefore, optional. Note that cross-reference lines on a complex schema tend to make the schema more difficult to read and should be omitted from the master schema. However, it is recommended that at least one unofficial copy of the schema have the cross-references noted.
8. If the schema designer wishes to display the groups by named area, an extended dashed line (alternating $\frac{1}{4}$-inch dashes with $\frac{1}{4}$-inch spaces) can be used to encircle the various areas. Even though the areas may be of irregular shape, the dashed lines should never cross each other (though relational and cross-reference lines may cross the area lines). The name of the area is inserted in the line in the same manner as the set name (see item 6). To avoid confusion, end each named area with "AREA" (e.g., CONTRACT-AREA).
9. Thus far in the II390 instructions no mention has been made of the use of colors to display the schema. This was intentional because of the reproduction problem. A schema with colors is suggested as a vehicle to clarify the master schema; however, leave all lines as dotted, dashed, etc.

DETAIL SYSTEM FLOWCHART—II400

Instructions

Form: Flowchart, G20.

Responsibility: Project Team Head.

Content: The Detail System Flowchart is an elaboration on the Proposed System General Flowchart, I80.

1. Use standard systems flowchart symbols.
2. Show all reports and documents (from System Reports and Documents, I40) and files and/or data bases in their proper relationship to one another.
3. Show manual or computer processes in the proper sequence. The flowchart can be organized and presented in a variety of methods. Select that which is most applicable (e.g., hierarchical, by subsystem activated by random events, by function, by minor and major cycles, by subsystems, or by a combination thereof). Few systems can be in straight sequential order. A modular approach is applicable in most cases.
4. Use the General Purpose form, G10, to explain the organization and presentation of the flowchart if other than simple sequential. Also use the G10 form where supplemental description is necessary to fully explain an operation, report, file usage, departmental interface, etc.
5. Add program ID's on all computer runs on on-line operations at the conclusion of Phase II, Part 1. A single processing symbol is used to depict a particular program in most cases.
6. Technique.
   a. Use ANSI flowchart symbols and abbreviations detailed in *Flowchart Symbols and Their Usage in Information Processing*, (ANSI, X3.5, 1970), American National Standards Institute, 1430 Broadway, New York, New York 10018.
   b. Use a pencil at all times. Final form flowcharts are also in pencil.
   c. Direction of flow is left to right and/or top to bottom when possible.
   d. Avoid long connecting lines by judicious use of on-page connectors.

e. Use a standard flowchart template when possible; however, symbols may be made larger or smaller as long as the symbol geometry is maintained.

f. Work with horizontal and vertical flow lines.

g. Number all symbols by placing a small number just outside the upper right corner of the symbol. The numbers should be consecutive between connected symbols when practical.

h. Place descriptive comments in each symbol and include an annotation if more space is required for an explanation. If the space for a single annotation is not sufficient, attach a G10 with further explanation. Circle the number just outside the upper right corner of symbol to denote that a further explanation is contained on the attached G10.

i. When they are not apparent, denote on-line and batch activities by placing "OL" or "BA," respectively, in the appropriate I/O or process block.

j. The grid on the back side of the flowchart form has vertical and horizontal lines which are spaced at 1-inch intervals. To draw a symbol, place the geometric center of the symbol at an intersection. Draw flow lines over the grid lines whenever possible.

7. Include the following on each Flowchart, G20.

a. Subsystem title. Descriptive title of subsystem (if applicable).

b. Total number of flowchart sheets used for the total system.

c. Page number of flowchart sheet.

DECISION TABLE—II410, II420

(Limited & Extended Entry)

Instructions

Forms: II410 and II420.

Responsibility: Project Team Head.

Content: The decision table is a vehicle that can be used to graphically illustrate what course or courses of action should be taken for all possible circumstances. The decision table can be produced as a supplement to a flowchart (either system or program) and, although not recommended, in some cases in lieu of a flowchart. The primary difference between documenting a procedure by flowcharts, written procedures, or decision tables is that flowcharts and written procedures leave the level of detail to the individual's discretion, but decision tables require that consideration be given to every alternative, option, condition, variable, etc. The decision table is appropriate for use in program and system logic design and documentation.

One decision table may or may not be sufficient to complete the logic for a given program or system. Each rule (or set of conditions) should end with an action that makes the rule complete or should be transferred to another decision table, which may be part of a network of decision tables.

There are two forms, II410 and II420, for the two types of decision tables. The Limited Entry Decision Table, II410, requires that complete condition and action descriptions be contained in their respective "stubs." The Extended Entry Decision Table, II420, allows for partial condition and action descriptions for the "stubs," with the remainder of the description being contained in the entry side. The only difference between the two forms is that more space is allowed for entries in the Extended Entry Decision Table. All item descriptions followed by "a" and "b" refer respectively to limited entry and extended entry only. Others refer to both.

1. System/program reference. That portion of the system for which the decision table is applicable. A formal name may not exist; therefore, a few descriptive words will suffice. Or, include the name of that program or program module for which the decision table is applicable. Enter the program name and identification, if applicable.
2. Title. An arbitrary title for the decision table. The title should be descriptive so that it indicates the type of decision illustrated on the decision table.

3. Condition stub. Condition labels are listed in this quadrant.
4. Action stub. Action labels are listed in this quadrant.
5. Condition entry. Condition entries are included in this quadrant.
6. Action entry. Action entries are included in this quadrant.
7. *a.* Condition label. All possible conditions pertinent to the table are listed.
   b. Partial condition label. Since condition label and entry must be combined to define a complete condition, only partial conditions are listed.
8. *a.* Condition entry. In any given square in the condition entries quadrant a "yes" (Y) or "no" (N) is entered to indicate the existence of the condition for a particular rule (a numbered column). A dash (—) may be used when a "yes" or a "no" for a particular condition has no bearing on actions to be taken for that rule.
   b. Condition entry. Note that more space is allotted for the Extended Entry Decision Table's condition entries. This allows for a word and/or symbol description to complement the partial condition label.
9. *a.* Action labels. All possible actions for any given rule are listed. If a network of decision tables is used, they are listed together by the action labels. A transfer from one table to another is accomplished by including "GO TO (table title)" in the action labels list. Include as many "GO TO's" as needed.
   b. Partial action labels. Since action label and entry must combine to define a complete action, only partial actions are listed. See 9a above for decision table networks.
10. *a.* Action entry. If a listed action is to be accomplished, place an "X" in the appropriate rule column and action line; otherwise, leave the square blank.
    b. Action entry. A word and/or symbol description to complement the partial action label.
11. Comments. Any explanatory comments should be placed here, and, if more space is required, additional comments should be placed on the back of the form.

REPORT TITLE	LIMITED ENTRY DECISION TABLE	NO. II410	DATE
SYSTEM TITLE			ID

SYSTEM/PROGRAM	(1)
TITLE	(2)

		1	2	3	4	5	6	7	8	9	10	11	12	13	14	15	16	17	18
A																			
B																			
C																			
D																			
E																			
F	(7a)									(8a)									
G																			
H																			
I																			
J																			
K																			
L																			
M																			
N																			
O	3	4																	
P	5	6																	
Q																			
R																			
S																			
T																			
U																			
V																			
W	(9a)									(10a)									
X																			
Y																			
Z																			
AA																			
BB																			
CC																			
DD																			

(11)

Comments

REPORT TITLE	EXTENDED ENTRY DECISION TABLE	NO. II420	DATE
SYSTEM TITLE			ID

SYSTEM/PROGRAM	(1)
TITLE	(2)

	(3)	(4) 1	2	3	4	5	6	7	8	9
A										
B										
C										
D										
E										
F	(7b)					(8b)				
G										
H										
I										
J										
K										
L										
M										
N										
O										
P	(5)	(6)								
Q										
R										
S										
T										
U										
V										
W	(9b)					(10b)				
X										
Y										
Z										
AA										
BB										
CC										
DD										

(11)

Comments

PRINTER LAYOUT—II430

Instructions

Form: II430.

Responsibility: Project Team Head.

Content: The purpose of the Printer Layout is to portray line or character printer-produced outputs in a format that a programmer can use in writing the program(s) necessary to produce the report or document. Proper spacing of report fields and heading information can be indicated by dummy characters and/or the actual headings.

1. Output title.
2. Output ID.
3. Output Description number. From Output Description, II340.
4. Space for labeling of lines, if appropriate.
5. Use this space to illustrate the report or document layout by indicating all heading information, maximum field sizes, etc., in the appropriate relative positions. For variable fields use the following dummy characters:

   N—Numeric only
   A—Alpha only
   X—Alphanumeric

   For edited output include the output "picture" with the appropriate special symbols [e.g., —, *, $, . (period), , (comma), etc.].

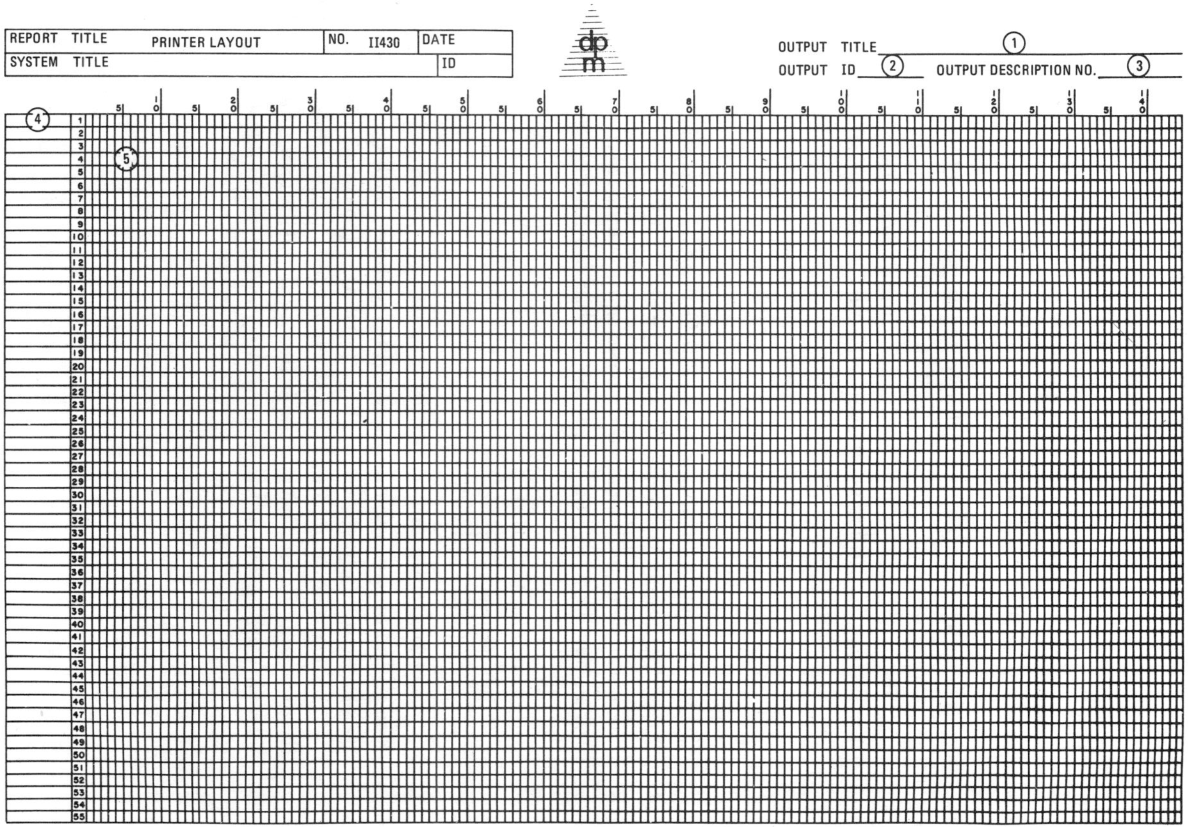

(actual size is 11" × 16")

CRT LAYOUT—II440

Instructions

Form: II440.

Responsibility: Project Team Head.

Content: The purpose of the CRT Layout is to portray a CRT display in a format that a programmer can use in writing the programs necessary to produce the display. Proper spacing of fields (input and/or output) and heading information can be indicated by dummy characters and/or actual headings.

1. Output title.
2. Output ID.
3. Output Description number. From Output Description, II340.
4. Space for labeling of lines, if appropriate.
5. Use this space to illustrate the layout of the video display by indicating all heading information, input and/or output field sizes, etc., in the appropriate relative positions. For variable fields use the following dummy characters:

   N—Numeric only
   A—Alpha only
   X—Alphanumeric

   For edited output include the output "picture" with the appropriate special symbols [e.g., —, *, $, . (period), , (comma), etc.].

   Indicate an input field by drawing a heavy black line under the dummy characters, which show the field position and length.
6. Use this space for notes, comments, and/or explanations that will help clarify the CRT layout.

REPORT TITLE CRT LAYOUT	NO. II440	DATE
SYSTEM TITLE		ID

OUTPUT TITLE ______ (1) ______

OUTPUT ID ___(2)___ OUTPUT DESCRIPTION NO. ___(3)___

(4)		5	10	15	20	25	30	35	40	45	50	55	60	65	70	75	80
	1																
	2																
	3	(5)															
	4																
	5																
	6																
	7																
	8																
	9																
	10																
	11																
	12																
	13																
	14																
	15																
	16																
	17																
	18																
	19																
	20																
	21																
	22																
	23																
	24																

(actual size is 11" × 16")

COMMENTS (6)

KEYPUNCH DESCRIPTION—II450

Instructions

Form: II450.

Responsibility: Project Team Head.

Content: The purpose of the Keypunch Description is to provide punching instructions for keypunch operators.

1. Card title. Brief descriptive title of card.
2. Card number. Supplied by data entry personnel for internal control.
3. Source document title. The document title from which the original data is taken.
4. Frequency. Frequency of job.
5. Volume. The average number of cards to be punched each time the job is completed and average number of keystrokes per card (e.g., 6000-40K/S).
6. Deadline. The day of the week, month, or cycle applicable, and time of day when the job is to be completed (e.g., by 16:00 on 5th day of monthly cycle).
7. Field number. Number fields for cross-reference with the source document(s).
8. Field name. Descriptive name of field (should correspond with the data element title if applicable).
9. Card columns. The beginning and ending character positions of the field, separated by a hyphen (e.g., 13–16).
10. Control. Indicate "D" for duplicate, "P" for punch, "S" for skip, and/or "V" for verify.
11. Alpha/numeric. Indicate "A" for alpha, "N" for numeric, and "A/N" for alphanumeric.
12. Instructions. Information regarding a particular field of data (e.g., left justify, zero fill, or pertinent word clarification). Take as many lines as necessary, up to four, for instructions and begin the next field number on the next full line.
13. Comments. Any additional comments necessary to complete the Keypunch Description.

Attach a copy of a source document to the Keypunch Description. Indicate on the source document the source position of each data field with a circled number that corresponds to the field number. This source document is part of the Keypunch Description.

REPORT TITLE KEYPUNCH DESCRIPTION	NO. II450	DATE
SYSTEM TITLE		ID

Card Title ______ ① ______ No. ______ ② ______

Source Document Title ______ ③ ______

Frequency ______ ④ ______ Volume ______ ⑤ ______ Deadline ______ ⑥ ______

Field No.	Field Name	Card Col.	Control	A/N	
⑦	⑧	⑨	⑩	⑪	⑫

Comments: ⑬

KEY-TO-DISK DESCRIPTION—II460

Instructions

Forms: General Purpose, G10; forms supplied by vendor of key-to-disk equipment.

Responsibility: Project Team Head.

Content: The purpose of the Key-to-Disk Description is to provide instructions for data-entry personnel. The form(s) and an instruction booklet are usually supplied by the vendor.

1. Use the General Purpose Form, G10, to include any special instructions to the data-entry supervisor or data-entry personnel.
2. For the purpose of uniformity of system documentation, attach a G10 to each vendor-supplied form.

SYSTEM CONTROLS—II470

Instructions

Form: General Purpose, G10.

Responsibility: Project Team Head.

Content: The purposes of the System Controls report are to identify and describe all system controls (both computer and/or manual) that are used to ensure accuracy and reliability.

1. Include controls procedures in both user organizations and the computer center.
2. Include descriptions, standardized forms, and instructions (if applicable) for the following system controls (as required):
    - *a.* I/O controls. Specify procedures to be performed for document counts, filing, logging, batching, corrections for erroneous data, checks for reasonableness, handling of classified material, etc.
    - *b.* Data reduction. Detail verification procedures.
    - *c.* Production schedule. Include procedures for deviation.
    - *d.* Librarian procedures. Specify logging and labeling procedures.
    - *e.* Logical security. Restrictions to system/data base access.

Note: The actual passwords and user ID's should not be maintained with the system documentation.

- *f.* Physical security.
- *g.* Administrative controls.

3. Attach a copy of each control log and an explanation of its use if necessary.

Note: Because of the significant overlap of accounting and EDP, auditors (internal and external) have been encouraged to consider EDP activity in their study and evaluation of accounting control. The PT should bear in mind that auditors may examine the system controls as part of their routine auditing function.

BACKUP PROCEDURES—II480

Instructions

Form: General Purpose, G10.

Responsibility: Project Team Head.

Content: The purpose of the Backup Procedures form is to define the backup and/or restart procedures in case of failure of the computer system and/or loss or damage to the data base. Include the following information:

1. Overall priority of system. If the computer goes down, other computer systems will also require attention. Indicate top, middle, or low priority relative to the other functional systems. Include an explanation, if applicable.
2. Location of primary backup site. Name of person in charge and telephone number. List the hardware and software differences at the backup site that would require making modifications prior to using the backup computer. Describe the action to be taken to overcome these differences.
3. Location of secondary backup site. Include the same information as in item 2.
4. Describe the logistics of transferring data, forms, etc., to the backup location.
5. Storage and security of backup files, listings, etc.
6. Frequency with which the various system files and/or data bases are copied.
7. Retention of backup files. Length of time that each backup file is maintained.
8. Other information pertinent to completing a description of backup procedures.

Note: System failure checkpoint/restart procedures are detailed in the Run Instructions, II590.

PROGRAM DESCRIPTION—II490

Instructions

Form: General Purpose, G10.

Responsibility: Project Team Head.

Content: The purposes of the Program Description are to identify and define each program and program segment required to automate the system as defined by the Detail System Flowchart.

1. Program title. A brief descriptive title.
2. Program label. The program label consists of six Alpha/Numeric characters used to designate a specific program and system. The first four numeric characters designate a specific program. The next two alpha characters designate the system and should be descriptive (e.g., "0001PR" for Payroll program number 1).
3. Type of programming language(s). Language(s) of program.
4. A narrative description of the program describing the tasks to be performed, the relationship to the rest of the system, files and/or data bases used, specific input, and specific output. Use standard nomenclature for reports, files, data elements, etc.
5. Frequency of processing [e.g., daily, weekly, on-line (specify up-hours), etc.].
6. Limitations and restrictions. Include specific limitations, restrictions, nonstandard processes or interfaces, and special requirements. Specifically:
   - *a.* Sequence of input data
   - *b.* Volume restrictions
   - *c.* Response time maximums
   - *d.* Primary storage limitations and/or requirements
   - *e.* Limitations on utility programs usage
   - *f.* Conflicts with standard operating practices for programming
   - *g.* Other
7. Detail specifications. Include the following as required:
   - *a.* Sorting, editing criteria
   - *b.* Arithmetic computations and logical manipulations
   - *c.* Tables required and how they will be established

d. Totals for controlling the system
e. Description of all parameters
f. Other program specifications

8. Required machine configuration. List the CPU type and components on which the processing will be performed. Be specific if more than one variety of a given component exists. Associate storage and I/O devices with specific reports and files (designate files as input and/or output). Note that this section can be completed before or after the program has been written.
9. List all program segments, subroutines, macros, and utility routines used by the program. Note that this section cannot be completed until after the program has been written.
10. List and define, by label, name, and description, each variable used in the program that is not included in the Data Element Matrix, II350 (e.g., TRAN1—Transaction counter, used to store running total of transactions). Note that this section cannot be completed until after the program has been written.
11. Job control specifications. If the program uses job control statements, list and explain each control statement. For each statement include the title (if applicable), a list of all fields by name or description, and their associated positions (if necessary). Include the actual field entry, if standard, or the optional entries and their effect on program execution.

    Use the following general format for each card:

	Card Title	Job Card	
Pos.	Field	Entry	Comments
1–2	std.	//	
3–5	std.	JOB	
6–11	Program ID	0020PR	
etc.			

    List the sequence of control statements in relation to each other, the program, and the data. Note that this section is to be completed after the program has been written.

12. Source listing. After the program is error-free and ready for production execution, append a source listing of the program to the Program Description.
13. Detail Program Flowchart. After the program is ready for production execution, append the Detail Program Flowchart, II550, to the Program Description.

Part 2—Programming

Work Flow Diagram—Phase II, Part 2

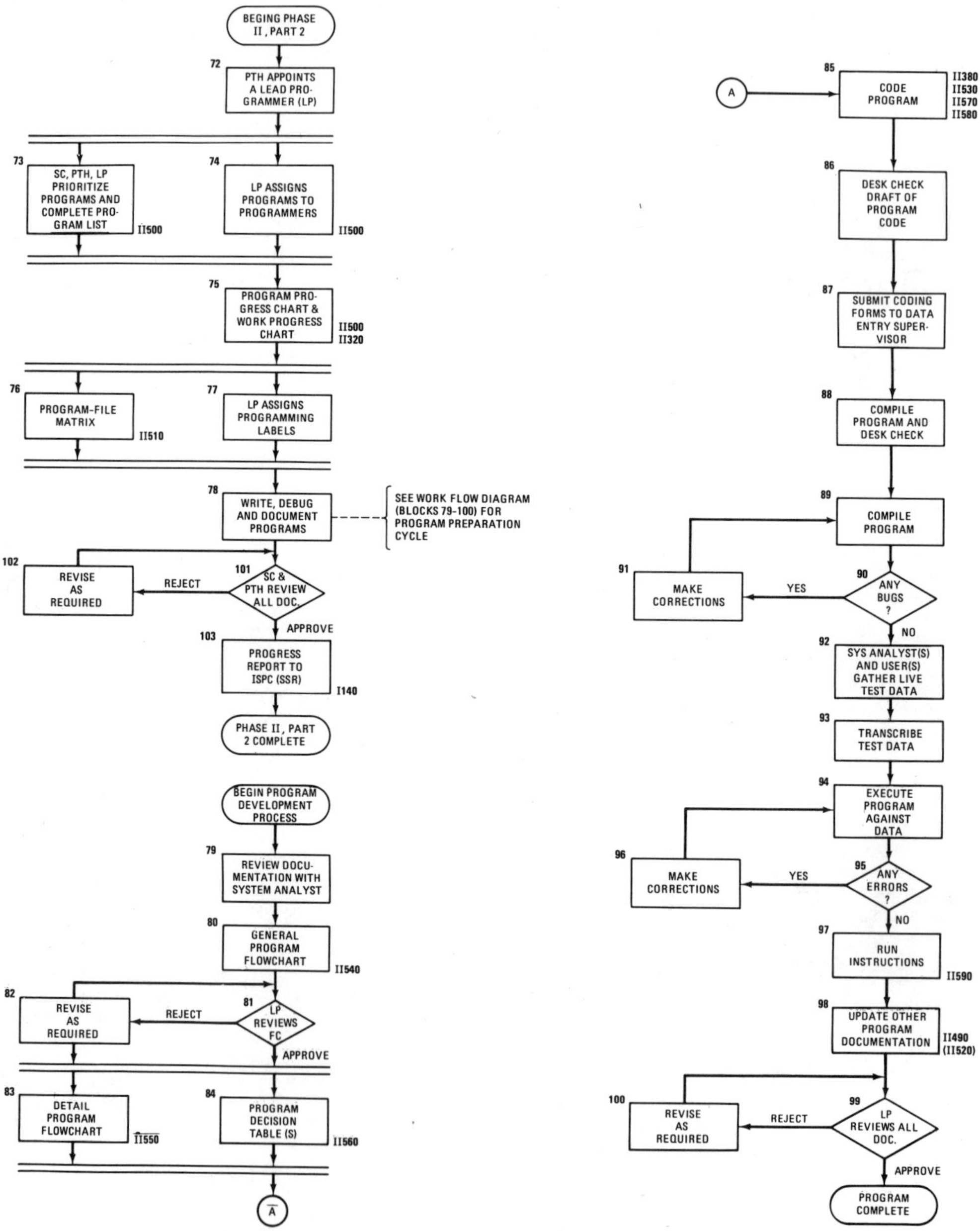

Block Descriptions—Phase II, Part 2

72. The PTH appoints, from the PT, a Lead Programmer. The Lead Programmer (LP) serves as a programmer/supervisor throughout the remainder of Phase II. When several programmers are involved in writing the systems program, one person must oversee the writing of the programs to ensure uniformity.

The LP should be expected to devote from 10% (project with two programmers on PT) to 50% (project with four or more programmers on PT) of his project time coordinating and scrutinizing the efforts of other programmers. The remainder of his time should be spent in production programming. In the case that only one programmer is assigned to the PT, the PTH serves as the LP.

73. The SC, PTH, and LP meet to prioritize the programs ("programs" is used to refer to programs or modules) in the order in which the coding is to be started. The LP then lists the program titles and labels on the Program Progress Chart, II500.

The SC, PTH, and LP should consider the following in prioritizing the programs:

a. The need for creation and maintenance of test files.

b. Program dependencies where one program requires all or part of another for execution.

c. The length and complexity of the program.

d. The fact that many smaller programs may require the same or more development time as one larger program.

e. Programs do not necessarily have to be written and/or completed in the order in which they are to be run in a production environment.

74. The LP in cooperation with the PTH assigns programmers to specific programs. The programmers are then associated, by name, with the appropriate program on the Program Progress Chart, II500.

In the selection process, consideration should be given to the programmers' general expertise, availability, and familiarity with the system.

75. The PTH and LP complete the preliminary items on the Program Progress Chart, II500. Included should be the percentage of the working day (on the average) that each assigned programmer is expected to work on the corresponding program and associated documentation. The estimated start and completion dates of the program and documentation should be included also.

The Program Progress Chart provides a graphic illustration of the status of any given program and is updated continuously by the LP as Phase II, Part 2 progresses.

The Work Progress Chart, II320, should be updated to reflect the more accurate time estimates for Phase II, Part 2.

76. The programmers of the PT complete the Program-File Matrix, II510. The purpose of the Program-File Matrix is to illustrate the relationship between the various programs and the files (or Data Bases) of the system.

77. The LP assigns programming labels for the data elements (use Data Element Matrix, II350) and the records (use File/Data Base Descriptions, II370). The same labels should be used throughout all system programs. The rules for labeling (naming) data elements, records, and files should be consistent with the programming language being used. If more than one language is used, labels should be created that are applicable to all programming languages used.

78. The general procedures for analysis, design, development, testing, and documentation of any given program are essentially standard. Therefore, a special work flow diagram is used to depict and describe the program development process. These steps are illustrated in Blocks 79 through 100 of the Phase II, Part 2 Work Flow Diagram. After all programs and documentation are complete, proceed to the next sequential block (101) in the main line Work Flow Diagram of Phase II, Part 2.

79. This activity is the first of a standard set of activities, which are to be accomplished during the development of any given program and associated documentation. This cycle of activities (79 through 100) pertains to each program.

The programmer gathers and reviews all documentation that is required to write and document the program. Depending upon the program requirements the list might include:

From Phase I

a. Applications Description, I10

b. System Design Constraints, I30

c. Glossary of Unique Terms, I100

From Phase II

a. Specific Output Descriptions, II340

b. Data Element Matrix, II350

c. Data Element Codes, II360

d. File/Data Base Descriptions, II370

e. Record Layouts, II380
f. Data Base Schema, II390
g. Detail System Flowchart, II400
h. Decision Tables, II410, II420
i. Printer Layouts, II430
j. CRT Layouts, II440
k. Keypunch Descriptions, II450
l. Key-to-Disk Descriptions, II460
m. System Controls, II470
n. Backup Procedures, II480
o. Program Descriptions, II490

After having reviewed the documentation, the programmer should discuss with the systems analyst(s) who prepared the documentation, and the UH if necessary, any questions that he might have concerning the objectives of the program.

80. The programmer completes the General Program Flowchart, II540. The purpose of the General Program Flowchart is to describe the major processing activities to be accomplished by the program and how they interrelate. A good general flowchart is a tremendous aid towards achieving an efficient and effective Detail Program Flowchart, II550, and ultimately a production program.

81. The LP reviews the General Program Flowchart, II540, examining the flowchart for ease of understanding, completeness, neatness, and sound logic, to ensure that the program, when complete, will accomplish the stated objectives. The LP either approves the flowchart or verbally requests that certain modifications be made.

82. The programmer makes the modifications requested by the LP and submits the revised General Program Flowchart, II540, to the LP for review.

83. The programmer completes the Detail Program Flowchart, II550. The purpose of the Detail Program Flowchart is to expand on the General Program Flowchart to include all calculations, data manipulation, logic operations, and input/output.

84. The programmer may use the Decision Tables, II410 and II420, as backup and support to (or, in some cases, in lieu of) the Detail Program Flowchart. See Program Decision Tables, II560, for instructions.

85. The programmer codes the program using generally accepted programming principles. In order to make spacing and transcription easier, programmers should use the COBOL Coding Form, II570, the FORTRAN Coding Form, II580, or commercially available standard coding forms for other languages, as applicable. Use the Record Layout, II380, and/or the Subschema Description, II530, as an aid to depict record layouts.

> *Note:* Interactive programming steps are similar but a programmer may elect not to use coding forms. Steps 86 through 88 are not required for interactive programming.

86. The programmer should thoroughly desk-check the initial draft of the program in order to ensure that all characters are legible and not subject to misinterpretation, that graphics are consistent, and that program syntax is correct. Comment statements that depict and describe the various logical sections of the program should be included now if they were not included earlier.

87. The programmer submits the completed source program on coding forms to the Data Entry Supervisor, accompanied by written instructions if required. The Data Entry Supervisor should place an internal priority on the job and relate an expected completion time to the programmer. The program is keypunched and verified by keypunch personnel. Upon completion, the Data Entry Supervisor notifies the programmer by telephone or in person as soon as possible. The programmer is responsible for the backup to the keypunched program.

88. The programmer compiles the program and receives a source listing of the program. After the first compilation, the programmer should desk-check the program for any logic errors and make changes as required.

89. The program is compiled in order to get a source listing with diagnostics.

90. If the program is free of diagnostics, the programmer proceeds in the program development process; otherwise he or she must make the necessary corrections.

91. The programmer makes the necessary corrections to the program.

92. Once the program is free of diagnostics, the programmer informs the PTH who in turn requests that the systems analyst(s) and the user representative(s) on the PT gather live test data for program testing. The responsibility for collection of the data rests with the PTH. The test data is submitted to the programmer in a meaningful format.

93. After compiling the data in a format consistent with that of the program, the programmer submits the test data to the Data Entry Supervisor for transcription to machine-readable format. The programmer should supply written instructions and/or Keypunch Descriptions, II450, and/or Key-to-Disk Descriptions, II460, as required. Upon completion, the Data Entry Supervisor should inform the programmer by telephone or in person as soon as possible.

94. The program is compiled and executed against test data.

95. Every branch of the program must be tested with the test data. The results are evaluated by the programmer, systems analyst(s) and user representative(s). If any errors in logic and/or output exist, the programmer must make the necessary corrections; otherwise, proceed with the program development process.

It should be noted that, in theory, every conceivable circumstance that could occur should be tested and the results evaluated with test data. If this were the case, then there would be no need to run in parallel during conversion. The programmer should strive to get all the bugs out, but invariably, a production parallel run during conversion frequently will reveal unnoticed errors.

96. The programmer makes the necessary corrections to the program.

97. The programmer completes the Run Instructions, II590, for the program. The purpose of the Run Instructions is to provide for the computer operators written instructions on how and when the program should be executed.

> *Note:* The revised Proposed System General Flowchart, I80, can be used by operations personnel to illustrate the interrelationship of all programs within the system.

98. Other program and system documentation should be updated, as required, to reflect any revisions made to the output specifications, files, records, etc. The Program Description, II490, also should be completed and updated.

> *Note:* The Schema Listing, II520, should be included with the Program Description for the Data Description Language.

99. The LP reviews all program documentation for ease of understanding, completeness, and neatness. The LP relates to the programmer any revisions to be made to the program documentation.

100. The programmer makes the necessary corrections to the program documentation.

101. The SC and PTH review all system documentation accumulated thus far for uniformity and completeness. The PTH relates to the appropriate PT member(s) any necessary revisions to the system documentation.

102. The PT members make the necessary revisions as required and submit the revisions to the scrutiny of the PTH and SC.

103. The PTH completes a System Status Report, I140, that reflects the completion of Phase II, Part 1 and the general progress of the project. The SSR and the Work Progress Chart, II320, are submitted to the ISPCH.

Documentation Instructions and Forms—Phase II, Part 2

PROGRAM PROGRESS CHART—II500

Instructions

Form: II500.

Responsibility: Project Team Head.

Content: The Program Progress Chart is a detailed supplement to the Work Progress Chart, II320, that indicates the order in which work on programs is to be accomplished and the progress towards completion of any given program ("program" refers to a program or a program module).

> *Note:* For preparation of the Program Progress Chart, consider the Schema Listing (DDL), II520, and Subschema Description(s), II530, as programs.

1. Program title. See Program Description, II490.
2. Program label. See Program Description, II490.
3. Programmer. The name(s) of the programmer(s) assigned to write and document the program.
4. Percent of time. The percentage of the working day (on the average) that the assigned programmers are expected to work on the corresponding program and associated documentation.
5. Two marks can be made in these boxes. As each numbered block activity (of the program preparation process) is begun, a diagonal (/) is placed in the appropriate box. After the activity is completed, the box is filled with an "X."
6. Estimated start date. Month, day, year (MM/DD/YY). The date on which work on the program and documentation is expected to begin. Make this estimate during the initial preparation of Form II500.
7. Actual start date. The date that work on the program and documentation is actually started.
8. Ahead/behind. The number of working days (based on a 5-day week, and at the established percent work commitment) behind or ahead after work is started on the program and documentation. Indicate status by placing the number of days ahead or behind in the appropriate box. Use "A" for ahead and "B" for behind (e.g., 5 days behind would be "5B").

9. Estimated completion date. The date on which the program and documentation is expected to be completed. Make this estimate during the initial preparation of Form II500.
10. Actual completion date. The date on which the program and documentation is actually completed.
11. Ahead/behind. Difference between actual and estimated completion dates. See item 8 for details.
12. Total number of sheets required to list all programs.
13. Sheet number.

Optional Gantt Chart Supplement (to the Program Progress Chart)

Form: Flowcharting Form, G20.

Content: The Gantt Chart Supplement to the Program Progress Chart provides a graphic time-phased display of the programming schedule as depicted on the Program Progress Chart.

1. Use the grid of the Flowcharting Form, G20, to draw the Gantt Chart. The top of the Gantt Chart can be the long or the short side depending on the number of programs and the estimated elapsed time. List the program titles down the lefthand side in either case.
2. Draw a line on the bottom of the chart and label it with months and days (circle Saturdays and Sundays). Again, use the grid when possible.
3. For each program draw a straight line adjacent to the program title, parallel to the bottom, and covering the estimated program development time (e.g., June 1 through July 14).
4. Actual start date. Indicate the actual start date for a particular program by placing an "S" over the line (or even with the line if prior to the estimated start date) and at the appropriate date.
5. Actual completion date. Indicate the actual completion date for a particular program by placing a "C" over the line (or even with the line if after the estimated completion date) and at the appropriate date.

REPORT TITLE PROGRAM PROGRESS CHART	NO. II500	DATE
SYSTEM TITLE		ID

Program Title	Label	Programmer	Percentage of Time	80 General F.C.	83 Detailed F.C.	85 Code Program	90 No Diagnostics	95 No Error/Data	99 Doc. Complete	Estimated Start Date	Actual Start Date	Ahead/Behind	Estimated Completion Date	Actual Completion Date	Ahead/Behind
(1)	(2)	(3)	(4)			(5)				(6)	(7)	(8)	(9)	(10)	(11)

PAGE (13) / (12)

PROGRAM-FILE MATRIX—II510

Instructions

Form: II510.

Responsibility: Lead Programmer (LP).

Content: The Program-File (and/or Data Base) Matrix illustrates the relationship between the programs and files of the system.

1. Program title. List all system programs in the same order as on the Program Progress Chart, II500. Include all programs, even those which do not interface with files.
2. Program label. As on the Program Description.
3. Data base/file title. As on Data Base/File Description, II370. Abbreviate if necessary. If appropriate, indicate a particular subschema, from Form II530, in lieu of the data base title. In these cases place "SS" by the subschema title to denote "subschema".
4. For those programs that utilize a given file, mark "I" for input only, "O" for output only, "I/O" for both input and output.
5. Total number of Program-File Matrix sheets required to list all programs.
6. Sheet numbers. If the allotted file space is insufficient, include supplemental sheet(s) with the same program titles and extend the list of files as required. Number these sheets 1a, 1b, 2a, 2b, 3a, 3b, and so on, when two sheets are required to list all files. Otherwise, number 1, 2, 3, and so on.

REPORT TITLE PROGRAM-FILE MATRIX	NO. II510	DATE
SYSTEM TITLE		ID

dpm

Data Base/File Titles

PROGRAM TITLE	LABEL							(3)										
(1)	(2)							(4)										

PAGE (6)/(5)

SCHEMA LISTING (DDL)—II520

Instructions

Form: General Purpose, G10.

Responsibility: Project Team Head.

Note: See Form II370, "Responsibility."

Content: The Schema Listing is simply the listing of the Data Description Language, DDL, used to describe the Data Base Schema, II390, for the data base management system. The Schema Listing serves as the permanent documentation of the schema and provides a vehicle for the data base administrator to make revisions to the schema.

Note: Most of the information contained in the listing is more easily discernible to the applications programmer in the Data Base Schema, II390.

On a General Purpose Form, G10, provide:

1. Schema title.
2. Data Description Language.
3. Any pertinent or explanatory information regarding the Schema Listing.

Note: The G10 header, "date", will reflect the latest update.

SUBSCHEMA DESCRIPTION—II530

Instructions

Form: General Purpose, G10 (11 × 16 inches).

Note: Complex subschemas may require a larger presentation area.

Responsibility: Lead Programmer (LP).

Content: The subschema is used to illustrate the data elements, records (groups), and relationships that an applications programmer requires for his use. The subschema, as the name implies, will use portions of the schema's data elements, and take on logical formats which may differ from the schema.

1. Refer to Data Base Schema instructions, II390, for Subschema Description instructions. The Subschema may be presented in the same manner as the Data Base Schema.
2. The Subschema Description may deviate from the Data Base Schema in several ways, depending upon the particular data base management system used. Each deviation should be clearly noted if it is not readily apparent to the subschema observer. Deviations, additions or deletions may be in:
   a. Authorizations
   b. Data elements elimination or sequence within groups
   c. Coding format of data elements
   d. Composite groups
   e. Key relationships
   f. Group sequencing
3. Attach a copy of the portion of the applications program that describes the subschema (Data Division in COBOL) to the Subschema Description, II530.

GENERAL PROGRAM FLOWCHART—II540

Instructions

Form: Flowcharting Form, G20.

Responsibility: Lead Programmer.

Content: The purpose of the General Program Flowchart is to describe the major processing activities to be accomplished by the program and how they interrelate. Detail should be only enough to show the flow of data through the program while identifying the logical segments of the program. The programmer can more easily work with a general flowchart to devise the best approach to writing the program.

See the Detail System Flowchart instructions, II400, item 6, for flowcharting technique guidelines.

Include the following on each flowcharting sheet:

1. Program title
2. Program label
3. Total number of flowcharting sheets used for this program
4. Page number of the individual flowcharting sheets

DETAIL PROGRAM FLOWCHART—II550

Instructions

Form: Flowcharting Form, G20.

Responsibility: Lead Programmer.

Content: The purpose of the Detail Program Flowchart is to expand on the General Program Flowchart to include all calculations, data manipulation, logic operations, and input/output. Be specific.

See Detail System Flowchart instructions, II400, item 6, for flowcharting technique guidelines.

Include the following on each flowcharting sheet:

1. Program title
2. Program label
3. Number of flowchart sheets used for this program
4. Page number of the individual flowchart sheets

PROGRAM DECISION TABLES—II560

Instructions

Forms: Limited and Extended Entry Decision Tables, II410 and II420.

Responsibility: Lead Programmer.

Content: See Forms II410 and II420, "Content".

1. In order to distinguish between systems- and programming-oriented decision tables, place a "P," for programming, after the "II410" and "II420" in the standard heading (e.g., II410P).

CODING FORMS—II570, II580

Instructions

Forms: II570 (COBOL), II580 (FORTRAN).

Responsibility: Lead Programmer.

Content: The COBOL and FORTRAN coding forms provide a spacing aid for programmers and keypunch operators during the coding and transcription stages, respectively, of program development. Refer to the appropriate programmer's guide for language syntax specifications. IBM COBOL (GX28-1464) and FORTRAN (GX28-7327) coding forms or other similar standardized forms are appropriate.

Use standard file, record, and data element names throughout the program. Use comment cards freely.

IBM

COBOL Coding Form –II570

GX28-1464-5 U/M 050*
Printed in U.S.A.

SYSTEM		PUNCHING INSTRUCTIONS	PAGE OF
PROGRAM		GRAPHIC	CARD FORM # *
PROGRAMMER	DATE	PUNCH	

SEQUENCE (PAGE) 1–3	(SERIAL) 4–6	CONT. 7	A 8	B 12 … COBOL STATEMENT … 72	IDENTIFICATION 73–80
	01				
	02				
	03				
	04				
	05				
	06				
	07				
	08				
	09				
	10				
	11				
	12				
	13				
	14				
	15				
	16				
	17				
	18				
	19				
	20				

*A standard card form, IBM Electro C61897, is available for punching source statements from this form. Instructions for using this form are given in any IBM COBOL reference manual. Address comments concerning this form to IBM Corporation, LDS Publishing, Dept. J04, 1501 California Ave., Palo Alto, Ca. 94304

*No. of forms per pad may vary slightly

IBM

FORTRAN Coding Form -II580

GX28-7327-6 U/M 050**
Printed in U.S.A.

PROGRAM		PUNCHING INSTRUCTIONS	GRAPHIC	PAGE OF
PROGRAMMER	DATE		PUNCH	CARD ELECTRO NUMBER*

COMM.	STATEMENT NUMBER	CONT.	FORTRAN STATEMENT	IDENTIFICATION SEQUENCE
1	2 3 4 5	6	7 8 9 10 11 12 13 14 15 16 17 18 19 20 21 22 23 24 25 26 27 28 29 30 31 32 33 34 35 36 37 38 39 40 41 42 43 44 45 46 47 48 49 50 51 52 53 54 55 56 57 58 59 60 61 62 63 64 65 66 67 68 69 70 71 72	73 74 75 76 77 78 79 80

*A standard card form, IBM electro 888157, is available for punching statements from this form

**Number of forms per pad may vary slightly

RUN INSTRUCTIONS—II590

Instructions

Form: II590.

Responsibility: Lead Programmer.

Content: The purpose of the Run Instructions is to provide computer operators with verbal and graphic instructions on how to set up and execute a particular program. Form II590 is contained on two pages. Completion of both pages is mandatory.

1. Program title.

2. Program label.

3. Name of the programmer who has primary responsibility for maintaining the program.

4. Home telephone number of the primary programmer.

5. Name of the programmer who has secondary responsibility for maintaining the program.

6. Home telephone number of the secondary programmer.

7. On-line/batch. Put "OL" for on-line or "BA" for batch.

8. Cycle. Run cycle, e.g., daily, weekly, etc. Indicate cycle relative to a particular benchmark day, if appropriate. For on-line systems, indicate days during week when system is up. If cycle is random simply put "as needed".

9. Operating hours. Put "NA" for batch and indicate daily operating hours (using 24-hour clock) for on-line systems (e.g., 0800-1700).

10,11,12. Output ID's. Indicate the CRT, printer and/or card outputs by ID. Preface each by "T" for CRT, "P" for printer, or "C" for card (e.g., P-0001PR01). Attach to the II590 a copy of each Output Description, II340, referenced. These Output Descriptions serve to supplement the Run Instructions.

13,14,15,16,17. Data base/file information on all files that are either input to or output from the program.

13. Data base/file title. Distinguish between temporary (transaction) and permanent files by placing a "(T)" by the temporary files.

14. Data base/file label.

15. Logical unit(s). The logical unit(s) on which the file resides.
16. Medium. Type of storage on which the file resides (e.g., card, magnetic tape, disk, etc.).

17. I/O. Note the file as providing input to the program, "I," modified created by the program, "O," or both, "I/O."
18. Run diagram. Using system flowcharting tecnniques, show all input and output relative to the CPU. Use specific I/O symbols and indicate the logical unit of the I/O's and the data base/file labels and/or output ID's, as appropriate, within each symbol. Output is denoted by an arrow directed from the CPU. Input is denoted by an arrow directed to the CPU. Input and output are noted by an arrow at each end of the information flow line.

    For on-line applications indicate terminal type, number of terminals, and location (if appropriate) of those which are interacting with a specific application program.
19. Include any special instructions to the operator on the reverse side of Form II590, page 1. Put "see reverse side" or "none" on the front side by special instructions, as appropriate.
20. The exact message(s) an operator may get on the console. Skip one line between each "message-action" explanation.
21. The action(s) that an operator should take following the appearance of the associated message on the console.
22. On a General Purpose Form, G10, detail the checkpoint/restart procedures required to begin system operation after system failure. If certain types of potential system failures can be identified and if restart procedures vary depending on the type of failure, detail the restart procedures for each type of system failure separately. Use graphical and/or word descriptions to detail the procedures.
23. Total number of pages of Form II590, pages 1 and 2.
24. Page number.

Note: The revised Proposed System General Flowchart, I80, can be used by operations personnel as an illustration of the interrelationships of all programs within the system.

REPORT TITLE RUN INSTRUCTIONS (part 1)	NO. II590	DATE
SYSTEM TITLE		ID

Program Title: (1) (2)

Programmers: 1. (3) Ph. (4) 2. (5) Ph. (6)

On Line/Batch: (7) Cycle: (8) Operator Hours: (9)

Output ID's (CRT, printer, card): 1. (10) 2. (11) 3. (12)

DATA BASE/FILE TITLE	LABEL	LOGICAL UNIT (s)	MEDIUM	I/O
(13)	(14)	(15)	(16)	(17)

Run Diagram:

(18)

CPU

Special Instructions: (see reverse side) (19)

Page (23) of (22)

REPORT TITLE RUN INSTRUCTIONS (part 2)	NO. II590	DATE
SYSTEM TITLE		ID

Program Title: ________ (1) ________ Label: ________ (2) ________

CONSOLE MESSAGES	OPERATOR ACTION
(20)	(21)

Page (23) of (22)

Part 3—Conversion and Implementation

Work Flow Diagram—Phase II, Part 3

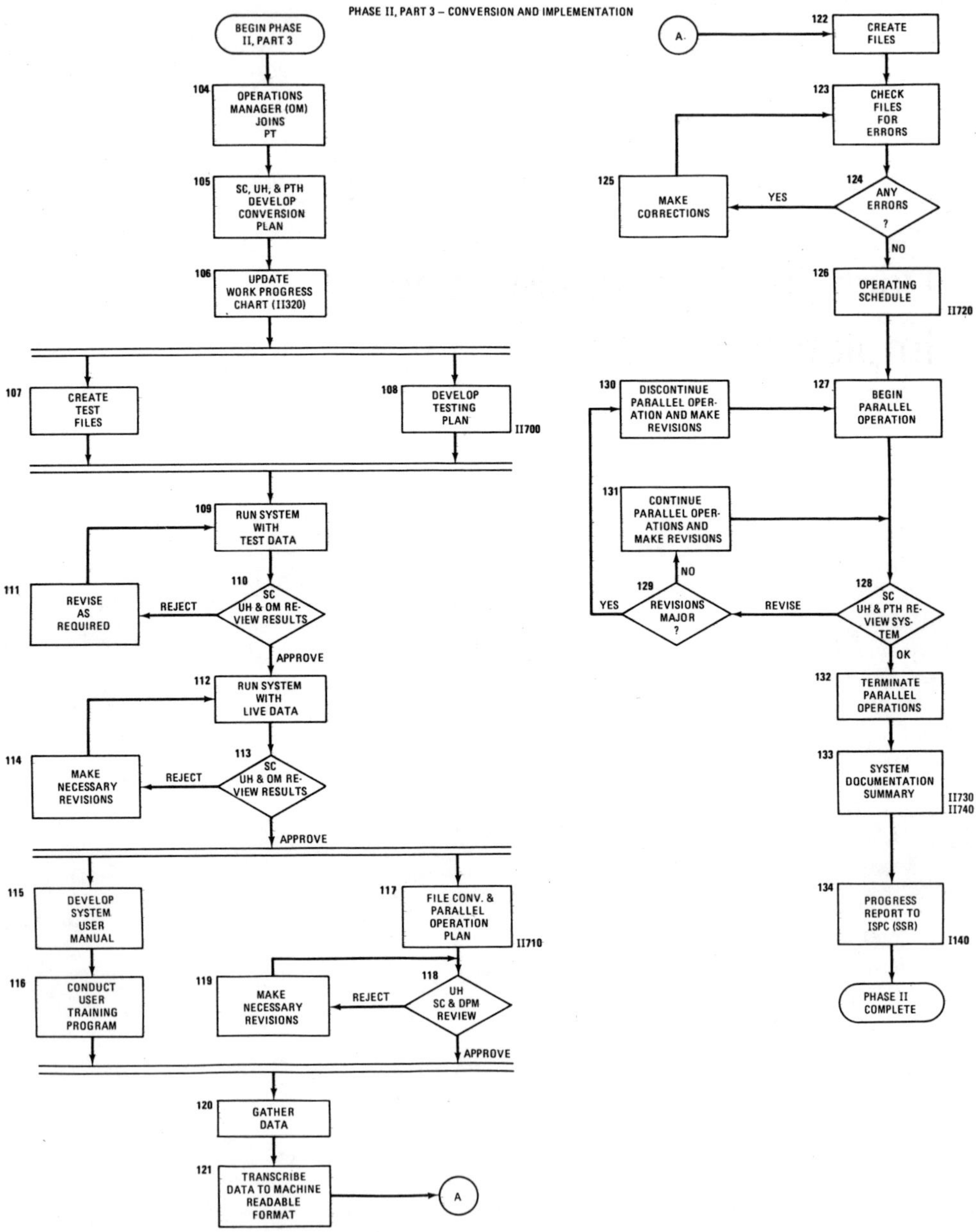

Block Descriptions—Phase II, Part 3

104. The Operations Manager (OM) joins the PT in order to have operations representation and expertise on the PT. The OM should not be a functionary on the PT in the sense of document and report preparation, but should serve in the capacity of consultant in the computer operations area. The PTH should request the presence of the OM at all subsequent meetings of the PT.

105. The SC, UH, and PTH meet to develop a general conversion plan. The PTH is responsible for calling the meeting and for preparing an informal written summary covering the major aspects of the system conversion and implementation process. The written summary should serve as an informal guideline for preparation of the more detailed Testing Plan, II700, and the File Conversion and Parallel Operation Plan, II710. Also, the summary should be useful in updating the Work Progress Chart, II320. The following information should be included:

a. Manpower allocations for user and DP
b. Time frame for each aspect of conversion and implementation
c. Resource allocation, e.g., use of computer time, etc.
d. Other general information pertinent to conversion

The written summary should be succinct yet general in nature.

106. Based on the results of the conversion plan meeting, the Work Progress Chart, II320, should be updated to coincide with the schedule depicted in the written results of the meeting.

107. The PT gathers data to create test files and/or test data base for testing systems. If possible, the records should be created from existing "real" records. This would make future testing with live data possible without recreating another set of test files. The test files should be sufficient in size to allow for a testing volume necessary to encompass the majority of possible circumstances that should occur.

108. The PT completes the Testing Plan, II700. The purpose of the Testing Plan is to define the process by which all systems and applications, software, files and/or data bases, and procedures can be integrated and validated using test data, then live data. The Testing Plan is a written report of the plan of action during the program and system testing stage of the system development process. The Testing Plan time schedule should coincide with that depicted on the updated Work Progress Chart, II320.

109. The first stage of testing should be by subsystem and/or cycle but should use test data supplied by the systems analyst(s) and user representative(s) on the PT. Test data should be judiciously compiled so all programs and system options and all error and validation routines are tested. The systems analyst(s) and user representative(s) of the PT are responsible for validating the results. The test should be repeated until all subsystems and/or cycles function properly. At this point, the entire system should be tested in the proper sequence. System testing should be repeated until the system functions properly.

> *Note:* The computer operators, using the Run Instructions, II590, are responsible for computer operation during system testing. This serves two purposes. First, the operators have an opportunity to become familiar with the system and, second, the operators can evaluate the Run Instructions for accuracy, completeness, and ease of understanding.

110. After program and system testing has been completed to the satisfaction of the PTH, the SC, UH, and OM review the results. Of particular interest should be the form of and information on reports, displays, and documents produced within the system; update procedures; and control and validation procedures. The SC, UH, and OM can either accept the test results or request that certain revisions be made. Any revisions at this stage of system development should be to "fine tune" the system, not to revamp the system.

111. The PT makes the necessary revisions to the system and updates the system documentation as applicable. Depending upon the extent of the revisions, the PTH may elect to test (with test data) all or part of the system in order to ensure that the programs and/or the overall system function properly.

112. The second stage of testing should also be by subsystem and/or cycle. Live data should be run against "real" records on the test files. The PT systems analyst(s) and user representative(s) are responsible for selecting live data from actual transactions in the existing system. Begin the test with a low volume of data and gradually increase the volume as the system is debugged until any given run would be likely to encounter most of the possible circumstances that might occur. If needed, augment live data with artificial transactions which are intended to test the extreme limits of quantities, sizes, etc.

> *Note:* "Real" data and records can be obtained by selecting backup master and transaction files at a particular point in time and transforming these to the format of the new system. There will, of course, be some manual transcription. When the project system is not automated, manual transcription may be the only alternative.

113. After program and system testing has been completed to the satisfaction of the PTH, the SC, UH and OM meet to review the results. Of particular interest should be the overall operation of the system including data collection, general operating procedures, and distribution of output. Unless unforeseen maladies appear, revisions, if any, should be minor and of a general nature.

114. The PT makes the necessary revisions to the system and updates the system documentation as applicable. Depending upon the extent of the revisions, the PTH may elect to test (with live data) all or part of the system, in order to ensure that the system functions properly.

115. The PT develops and compiles a system user manual. Included should be:

a. The objectives of the system
b. Brief description of the overall system
c. Instructions for completing and/or understanding forms, reports, or documents
d. Instructions for remote inquiry and/or update if applicable
e. Data collection, update, and/or distribution procedures
f. Flowcharts, if appropriate, to describe the general user operating procedures
g. Other information pertinent to user understanding and operation of the system

Since all of the above listed information is included in the system documentation, the system user manual need not be included in the permanent documentation package. However, the system user manual should be updated as required. The update responsibility rests with the SC after system implementation since the SC has responsibility for maintaining all documentation.

116. The PT conducts user training program(s) for all users who either assist in the operational aspects of the system or make use of the system output. A training program should include:

a. Purpose and objectives of the system
b. Differences between the existing and the new systems
c. Overview of system operation and procedures
d. Organization and use of the system user manual
e. Duties and responsibilities of user and DP personnel
f. Other information pertinent to user understanding and operation of the system

117. The PT completes the File Conversion and Parallel Operation Plan, II710. The File Conversion and Parallel Operation Plan is a written report of the plan of action for the critical file conversion and parallel operation stages of system implementation. Conversion and implementation is a system itself.

118. The PTH calls a meeting of the DPM, SC, and UH for the purpose of reviewing the File Conversion and Parallel Operation Plan, II710. The DPM, SC, and UH either accept the plan or make recommendations for revisions to the plan.

Upon acceptance of the plan, the PTH should update the Work Progress Chart, II320, to coincide with the time schedule depicted in the plan, if needed.

119. The PT makes the necessary revisions to the File Conversion and Parallel Operation Plan, II710, and submits the revised plan to the scrutiny of the DPM, SC, and UH.

120. In preparation for a complete file conversion from existing files or raw data, the PT accumulates the required data. All data must be in a format that is consistent with that of the new system. There should be no backlog in updating.

121. The data and files are transcribed into a machine-readable format and verified for accuracy.

122. The system files or data bases are created by the PT. All data and files are transferred to the appropriate storage media.

123. After each file (or data base) is converted, the records should be printed out in a format that can most easily be sight-checked for accuracy and in an order that is consistent with that of the original documents. The users, with assistance from the PT, are responsible for verifying the accuracy of the files. This can be accomplished by several methods. First, the user can visually check each data element; however, this is recommended for relatively small files only, since this is a vigilance task where inspector accuracy is low. Second, the user can visually check selected records according to a preconceived scheme (e.g., every third or every tenth record). The user should record all errors by record. The PTH, upon receiving the errors, should evaluate the file errors for patterns (e.g., all company customers with 28015 zip codes should be 18015).

Depending upon the size of the file, the PT may elect to run against the file specialized programs that check for inordinately high and/or low values of particular data elements. This may be done before and/or after users' visual checks.

It should be noted that the time phasing of the file conversions is critical since any new transactions require that updates be made to both the existing and the newly created files in order to continue present operations and provide up-to-date files for use by the new system. Therefore, the expected elapsed time between file conversion and parallel operation should be kept to a minimum.

124. If user or DP personnel find any errors in any given file, the file must be corrected and rechecked.

125. The PT, in cooperation with operations personnel, should use the appropriate system for updating programs to make the correct entries to the file(s) in error.

126. The PT completes the Operating Schedule, II720. The purpose of the Operating Schedule is to describe the time frame for the delivery of the source data to DP and the subsequent transcription of data and/or reports to the users. This report is mainly for batch-oriented systems, but is also applicable for on-line systems that require a physical transfer of data, reports, documents, etc., between user and DP locations.

127. The parallel operation, a cooperative effort between user and DP personnel, begins in accordance with the File Conversion and Parallel Operation Plan, II710.

128. The SC, UH, and PTH meet daily, or as required, during parallel operation in order to evaluate the system. The PT members have the responsibility of personally monitoring the details of system operation. Should any member find any problem areas or potential problem areas in the system operation, the problems should be brought to the attention of the PTH who, in turn, presents the problems to the SC and UH. They make a decision as to the severity of the problem and direct what action should be taken.

The parallel operation should continue, as a rule of thumb, through at least one major cycle (e.g., 1 month for monthly payroll, but not to continue through quarterly and year-end reporting) under the continuous scrutiny of the SC, UH, and PTH. At any time subsequent to the successful completion of one cycle, the SC, UH, and PTH may collectively recommend the termination of parallel operation, leaving only the new system in full operation.

129. After the SC, UH, and PTH have recommended that revisions and/or corrections be made to the system, they must then assess the extent of the revisions relative to the ongoing system operation. If the revisions and/or corrections are major in scope, a recommendation might be made to terminate parallel operation; however, if revisions and/or corrections are deemed minor in scope and can be made without having any substantial effect on the parallel operation, a recommendation might be made to continue parallel operation and make the necessary revisions and/or corrections.

130. Parallel operation is terminated because of the scope of the required revisions to the system; however, unless the revision time exceeds one major cycle, the new system files should be updated and maintained until the restart of parallel operations. If parallel operations are discontinued for a considerable length of time and new system files maintenance is infeasible, restart should begin with recreating the files (Block 120). After the revisions have been made and approved, the PT should update the system documentation to reflect the changes.

131. The PT makes the necessary revisions to the system during the continuation of parallel operations. After the revisions have been made and approved, the PT should update the system documentation to reflect the revisions.

132. The final approval of the new system by the SC, UH, and PTH is the signal for the turnover of the new system to the user and the termination of parallel operations.

133. The PTH accumulates the system documentation and completes the System Documentation Summary, II730, and the System Development Documentation Summary, II740. The former serves as a cover for the system documentation required for system maintenance and update, and the latter serves as a cover for all other system documentation.

134. The PTH completes a System Status Report, I140, that reflects the completion of Phase II and other information pertinent to the project progress. The SSR and the completed Work Progress Chart, II320, are submitted to the ISPCH.

Documentation Instructions and Forms—Phase II, Part 3

TESTING PLAN—II700

Instructions

Form: General Purpose, G10.

Responsibility: Project Team Head.

Content: The Testing Plan is a written report of the plan of action during the program and system testing stage (Blocks 109 through 114) of system development. The Testing Plan can be divided into cycles and/or subsystems and/or general phases, as applicable. In any case, the breakdown, if any, should be defined in a manner and in terminology acceptable to both users and DP personnel. Discuss who is responsible for what, when (names of personnel, duties, and time frame) and, if applicable, where.

The Testing Plan should define the process by which all systems and applications software, files and/or data bases, and procedures can be integrated and validated using test data, then live data.

FILE CONVERSION AND PARALLEL OPERATION PLAN—II710

Instructions

Form: General Purpose, G10.

Responsibility: Project Team Head.

Content: The File Conversion and Parallel Operation Plan is a written report of the plan of action for the critical file conversion and parallel operation (some new systems will not require a parallel operation period) stage of system development (Blocks 120 through 132). The plan should be a detailed description of all time frames and deadlines and of user and DP personnel duties and responsibilities. The description should be completed in a manner and in terminology acceptable to both user and DP personnel.

OPERATING SCHEDULE—II720

Instructions

Form: General Purpose, G10.

Responsibility: Project Team Head.

Content: The purpose of the Operating Schedule is to describe the time frame for the delivery of source data to DP, the subsequent transcription of the data, the actual processing, and the delivery of computer-produced documents and/or reports to the users. For batch systems, specify the day (relative to a specific cycle, if applicable, e.g., 3rd day of weekly cycle) and time (using 24-hour clock, e.g., 1400 instead of 2:00 P.M.) by which:

1. The source data must be delivered to DP (define source).
2. The source data must be transcribed and verified into machine-readable format.
3. The processing necessary to produce a given output is to be completed.
4. The output is to be delivered to the user (name user(s)).

For on-line systems, also specify the operating hours of the systems.

Include other information, as required, that is pertinent to compiling a complete description of the operating schedule.

SYSTEM DOCUMENTATION SUMMARY—II730

Instructions

Form: II730.

Responsibility: Project Team Head.

Content: The System Documentation Summary serves as a cover for the system documentation required for system maintenance and update. The documentation should be included in a three-ring binder and in the order listed on Form II730. Dividers labeled Phase I; Phase II, Part 1, Phase II, Part 2, Phase II, Part 3; and Phase III should be inserted at the appropriate locations. Phase III documentation should be included as it becomes available.

1. Put either "X," to denote inclusion, or "NA," to denote not applicable.
2. Multiple use can be made of this document. Put the total number of unique documents (e.g., for 13 Output Descriptions, II340, put "13," or put "NA").
3. Put the number of programs in the system. Include the program documentation by program in the order listed in the Program-File Matrix, II510.
4. Signature of DPM.
5. Signature of SC.
6. Signature and position of PTH.
7. Signatures and positions of PT members. Note department and/or division if other than DP.

REPORT TITLE	SYSTEM DOCUMENTATION SUMMARY	NO. II730	DATE
SYSTEM TITLE			ID

Phase I	–	Initiation and Feasibility Study Phase	
I10	–	Applications Description	(1)
I20	–	Definition of Proposed System	(1)
I30	–	System Design Constraints	(1)
I80	–	Proposed System General Flowchart	(1)
Phase II, Part 1	–	System Analysis and Design	
II330	–	Output Reference List	(1)
II340	–	Output Descriptions	(2)
II350	–	Data Element Matrix	(1)
II360	–	Data Element Codes	(2)
II370	–	File Descriptions	(2)
II380	–	Record Layouts	(2)
II390	–	Data Base Schema	(1)
II400	–	Detail System Flowchart	(1)
II410-II420	–	Decision Tables	(2)
II430	–	Printer Layouts	(2)
II440	–	CRT Layouts	(2)
II450	–	Keypunch Descriptions	(2)
II460	–	Key-to-disk Descriptions	(2)
II470	–	System Controls	(1)
II480	–	Backup Procedures	(1)
Phase II, Part 2	–	Programming	
II510	–	Program-File Matrix by Program:	(1)
II490	–	Program Description	(3)
II540	–	General Program Flowchart	
II550	–	Detail Program Flowchart	
II560	–	Decision Tables	
II590	–	Run Instructions	
II520	–	Schema Listing (DDL)	(1)
II530	–	Subschema Description	(2)
Phase II, Part 3	–	Conversion and Implementation	
II720	–	Operating Schedule	(1)
Phase III	–	Evaluation and Ongoing Operation	
I120	–	Cost Report (Final)	(1)
III900	–	Postimplementation System Evaluation	(1)
III910	–	Review Schedule	(1)
III920	–	Summary of Periodic Review	(1)

Data Processing Manager (4) ____________________

Systems Coordinator (5) ____________________

Project Team Head (6) ____________________

Project Team Members (7) ____________________

____

____

____

____

SYSTEM DEVELOPMENT DOCUMENTATION SUMMARY—II740

Instructions

Form: II740.

Responsibility: Project Team Head.

Content: The System Development Documentation Summary serves as a cover for the system documentation package not required for system maintenance and update. This documentation should be included in a three-ring binder and in the order listed on Form II740.

1. Put either "X," to denote inclusion, or "NA," to denote not applicable.
2. Multiple use can be made of this document. Put total number of unique documents (e.g., for 3 SSR's, I140, put "3," or put "NA").

REPORT TITLE SYSTEM DEVELOPMENT DOCUMENTATION SUMMARY	NO. II740	DATE
SYSTEM TITLE		ID

I 40 –	System Reports and Documents	①
I50 –	System Data Files	①
I60 –	System Data Elements	①
I70 –	Present System General Flowchart	①
I90 –	Scope of System Development	①
I110 –	Benefits Report	①
I120 –	Cost Report	②
I140 –	System Status Reports	②
II300 –	Estimated Personnel Requirements	①
II310 –	Personnel Training Requirements	①
II320 –	Work Progress Chart	②
II700 –	Testing Plan	①
II710 –	File Conversion and Parallel Operation Plan	①

6

Phase III—Evaluation and Ongoing Operation

Work Flow Diagram—Phase III

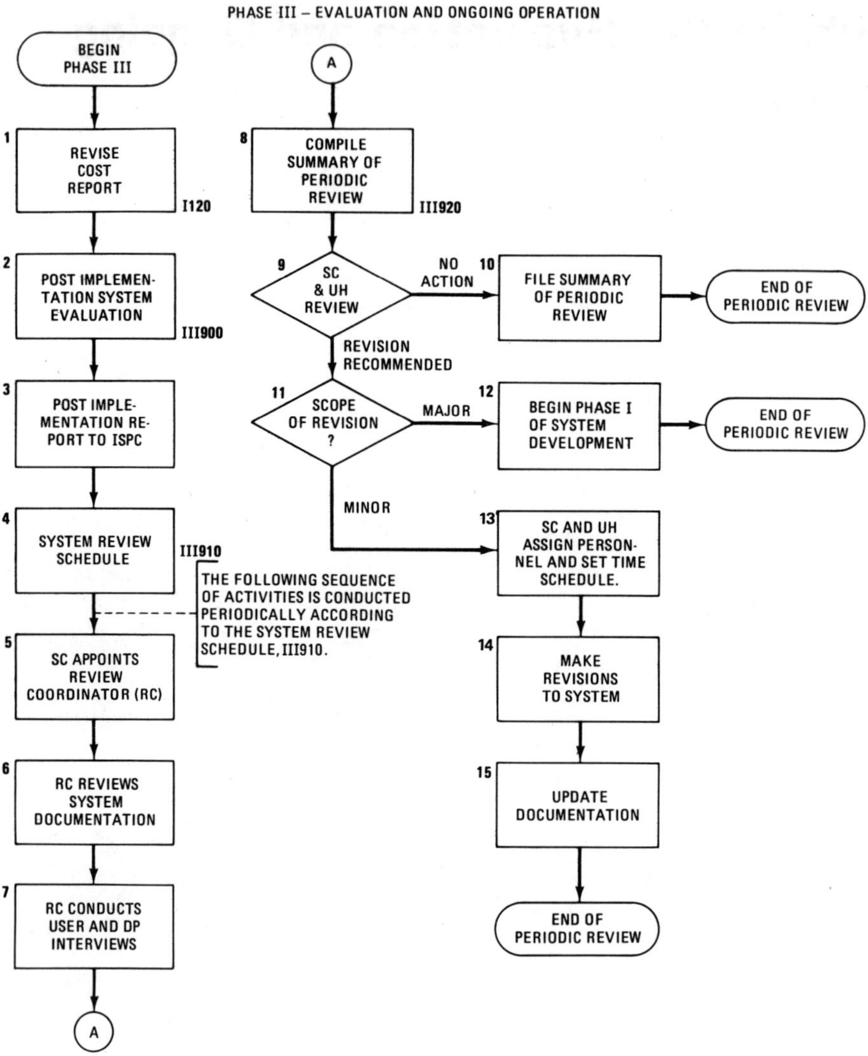

Block Descriptions—Phase III

1. The PTH should revise the Cost Report, I120, to reflect the final system development costs for Phases I and II, and the ongoing costs for system operation. The PTH should coordinate with the UH in order to gather the required data for completion of the Cost Report.

> *Note:* Accurate and consistent cost data may not be available until at least 1 month after implementation; therefore, this activity should not begin until such time.

2. The PTH completes the Postimplementation System Evaluation, III900. This evaluation is a critical examination of the system by the PTH that is to be completed not earlier than 3 months or later than 6 months after Phase II termination. After completion of the evaluation, the PTH submits the Cost Report, I120, and the Postimplementation System Evaluation to the ISPCH.

3. The PTH should give an oral presentation to the ISPC at the next scheduled meeting after the delivery of the Postimplementation System Evaluation to the ISPCH. This presentation should include a summary of both the Cost Report, I120, and the evaluation, III900.

During this meeting, the ISPC establishes the system review cycle (the elapsed time between each system review). The system review cycle should be set at not less than 3 months nor more than 1 year.

4. The PTH completes the System Review Schedule, III910. The System Review Schedule is the formal document from which reviews are scheduled and are properly logged following each periodic review.

5. The SC is responsible for initiating the periodic system reviews in accordance with the System Review Schedule, III910. Approximately 2 weeks prior to the review date, the SC should assign a systems analyst who is familiar with the system (former PT member, if possible) to conduct the review. The systems analyst is then called a review coordinator (RC) and is given the authority to conduct the review. The SC still has the responsibility for successful completion of the review.

6. The Review Coordinator (RC) becomes familiar with the System Documentation Summary, II730.

7. The RC conducts interviews with DP personnel (in particular, operational personnel) and user personnel from clerks to UH. The interviews should center around the questions of system efficiency and effectiveness and/or how the system can be improved. Such topics as turnaround, response time, relevance of information, distribution, forms and other output

formats, organization of records, files and data bases, system controls and validation procedures, update and backup procedures, suggestions for improved system performance, currency of system documentation, and other pertinent topics should be discussed, as appropriate, during the interview sessions.

8. The RC completes the Summary of Periodic Review, III920. This review summary provides a permanent record of the results of the interviews and the recommendations of the RC.

9. The SC and UH review the Summary of Periodic Review, III920. The RC's recommendations are to be used as guidelines for the SC and UH. The SC and UH can either table the review with no action being taken or recommend that certain revisions be made to the system. If their revisions are different from those recommended by the RC, the SC and UH should communicate their recommendations to the RC, and the RC should update the Summary of Periodic Review to reflect the joint recommendations of the SC and UH.

10. The SC and UH recommend that no action be taken. The Summary of Periodic Review, III920, is then filed permanently as part of the System Documentation Summary, II730. The periodic review is then complete.

11. The SC and UH categorize the scope of the system revision as being either minor (requiring less than 3—arbitrary by company—professional man-weeks) or major. Minor revisions can be made with the joint consent of the SC and UH and under the direction of the SC. Major revisions must be submitted to the scrutiny of the DPM and/or the ISPC.

12. If the scope of the system revision is deemed major by the SC and UH, the user must prepare an Applications Description (AD), I10, based on the Summary of Periodic Review. This block then becomes Block 1, Phase I or the beginning of the system development process.

13. The SC and UH assign personnel to make the required system revisions and establish a time schedule for development and implementation. The SC should coordinate the revisions project.

14. The system revisions should be made by the assigned personnel using the Work Flow Diagrams for the system development process as required.

15. The SC is responsible for ensuring that all appropriate system documentation is updated to reflect any system revisions.

Documentation Instructions and Forms—Phase III

POSTIMPLEMENTATION SYSTEM EVALUATION—III900

Instructions

Form: General Purpose, G10.

Responsibility: Project Team Head.

Content: The Postimplementation System Evaluation is a critical examination of the system by the PTH. The purpose of the evaluation is not to recommend or appraise an individual's performance, but to appraise the operational aspects of the system. Included should be some mention of the following:

1. Comparison of actual and anticipated performance at the completion of Phase I
2. Discussion of the extent to which the system accomplished stated objectives
3. Discussion of any unexpected benefits derived from the system
4. A candid and detailed discussion any mistakes made by either user or DP personnel during the system development process and how those mistakes could have been avoided
5. Other information pertinent to an evaluation of the overall system

SYSTEM REVIEW SCHEDULE—III910

Instructions

Form: III910; General Purpose, G10.

Responsibility: Project Team Head.

Content: A predetermined periodic review schedule encourages both user and DP personnel to be active in initiating needed system revisions and to be responsive in implementing these revisions. The System Review Schedule is the formal document from which reviews are scheduled and are properly logged following each periodic review.

1. System review cycle. A set period of time that elapses between the beginning of reviews (e.g., quarterly, semiannually, etc.). The review cycle should be not less than 3 months or more than 1 year.
2. Review date. The beginning date of each review. The review dates should be filled in at least 2 years in advance.
3. The name of the Review Coordinator (RC).
4. The beginning and ending dates during which the system was reviewed.
5. Action taken. Either put "none" or "revised." If the system was revised in any way, attach a brief description of the revisions to this form. Use the General Purpose, G10, and identify it with a specific periodic review by including the review date on the G10.

REPORT TITLE SYSTEM REVIEW SCHEDULE	NO. III910	DATE
SYSTEM TITLE		ID

SYSTEM REVIEW CYCLE ______ (1) ______

REVIEW DATE	REVIEW COORDINATOR	DATES REVIEWED	ACTION
(2)	(3)	(4)	(5)

SUMMARY OF PERIODIC SYSTEM REVIEW—III920

Instructions

Form: General Purpose, G10.

Responsibility: Review Coordinator (RC).

Content: The Summary of Periodic System Review provides a permanent record of the results of the review and the recommendations of the Review Coordinator. The following information should be included as applicable:

1. Assigned review date. The date on which the review was to begin (from System Review Schedule, III910).
2. Actual review dates. The dates during which the review was conducted.
3. Overall status of the system. Include all appropriate remarks by user and DP personnel about timeliness, clarity, applicability, format, response or turnaround time, reports, documents, and/or displays.
4. Recommended action. Description of recommended actions based on the results of the periodic review.
5. Benefits to be derived from the above actions, if any.

7

General Reports

Introduction

The three reports contained in this chapter are not peculiar to any phase or part of the system development process, but are applicable throughout the entire process.

The General Purpose Form, G10, is simply a blank form with a standard header that is used for text and graphics reports and documentation. The report form has both a standard $8\frac{1}{2} \times 11$-inch size and a 16×11-inch fold-out size.

The Flowcharting Form, G20, provides the programmer and analyst with a vehicle for accomplishing flowchart work in a neat and standardized format while retaining the flexibility necessary in flowcharting. Note that guidelines are drawn on the reverse side of the form.

The Document Revision Log, G30, is used by the Systems Coordinator to log all revisions to an operational system.

Documentation Instructions and Forms—General

GENERAL PURPOSE FORM (GP)—G10

Instructions

Form: G10 ($8\frac{1}{2} \times 11$-inch) and (11×16-inch, with $11 \times 7\frac{1}{2}$-inch fold on the right side).

Responsibility: NA.

Content: The General Purpose form is the basic form used for many nonstandard documents. The use of the GP form will be specified where applicable. When typing the material on each page, use the following as minimums for margin allowances:

From bottom of page label—1/2 inch
From left side of page—1 inch
From bottom of page—1 inch
From right side of page—1/2 inch

1. Title of report for which the GP is used.
2. Number of report for which the GP is used.
3. The date on which all system documentation was completed for this system. If the document is revised after this date, the date then becomes the revision date and is preceded by "rev" for revised (e.g., rev 10/15/79).
4. Title of system.
5. Associated system identification. Two letter system identifier.
6. Indicate page number of report and total number of pages in the report. For example, first of five pages would be noted as "1/5."

REPORT TITLE (1)	NO. (2)	DATE (3)
SYSTEM TITLE (4)	ID (5)	PAGE (6)

GENERAL PURPOSE FORM (GP)
FORM NO. G10

FLOWCHARTING FORM—G20

Instructions

Form: G20.

Responsibility: NA.

Content: The Flowcharting Form serves as an aid to programmers, systems analysts and users engaged in program and/or system flowcharting. Vertical and horizontal lines at 1-inch intervals are supplied as guidelines by which to place symbols and flow lines.

1. Do actual flowcharting on the header side of the G20. The grid lines should be on the back side.
2. Center symbols on the flowcharting template on both a vertical and a horizontal grid line.
3. Do not violate the perimeter on the front side.
4. See Form II400 instructions for details on flowcharting techniques.

REPORT TITLE	FLOWCHARTING FORM	NO. G20	DATE
SYSTEM TITLE		ID	PAGE

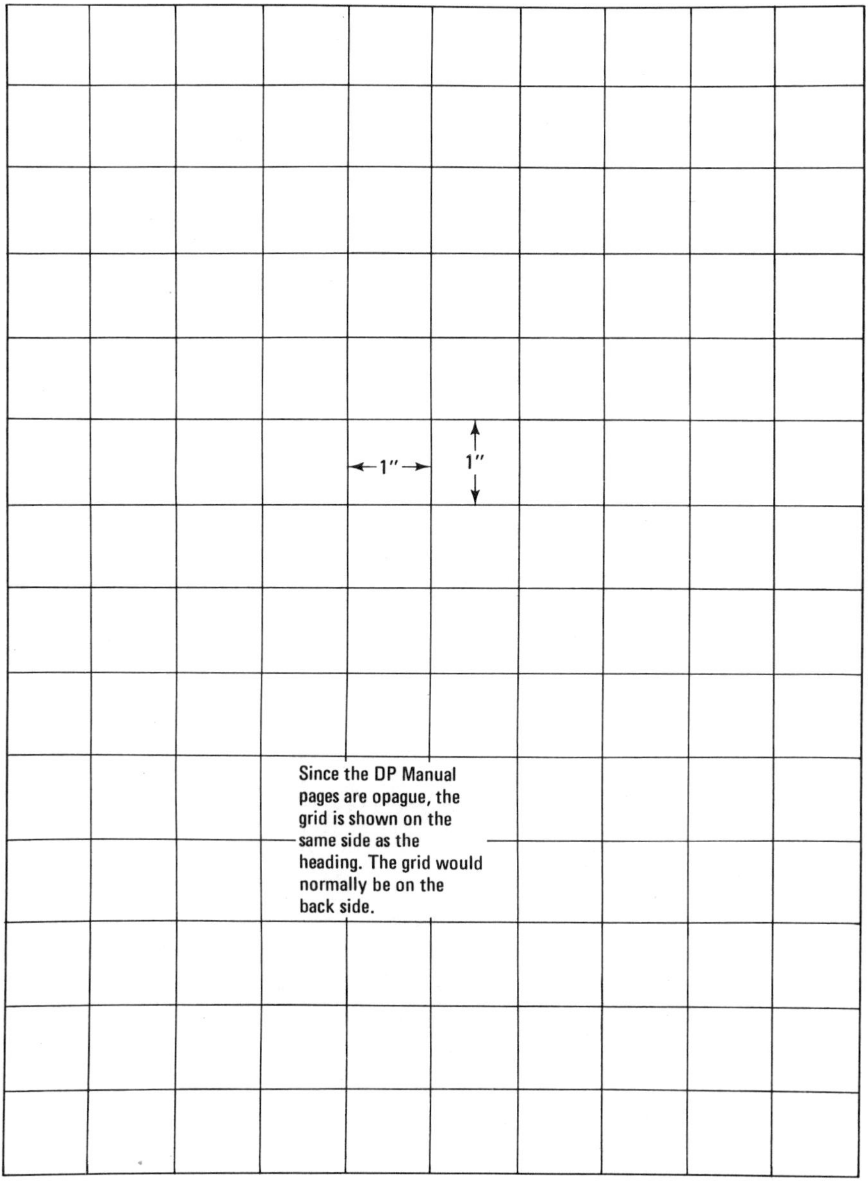

(Actual size is 10″ x 14″)

DOCUMENT REVISION LOG—G30

Instructions

Form: G30.

Responsibility: Systems Coordinator.

Content: The Document Revision Log is provided as a standard mechanism for recording revisions to existing system documentation. It is maintained only after the completion of Phase II documentation. The following information is included for each change:

1. Title of document that is revised.
2. Number of document that is revised. Include page number, if applicable.
3. Date—month, day, and year of revision.

A Form G30 is included with the permanent system documentation following Phase II. Revisions should be logged on the G30 by the SC as they occur. Any revised document should reflect the month, day, and year in which it was revised in the "date" box of the standard corporate heading (e.g., rev 10/15/79).

REPORT TITLE DOCUMENT REVISION LOG	NO. G30	DATE
SYSTEM TITLE	ID	PAGE

DOCUMENT TITLE	NUMBER	DATE OF REVISION
(1)	(2)	(3)

III

General Computer Center Documentation

8

Hardware Documentation: Computer, Peripherals, Communications

Introduction

Every computer center, regardless of size, should have and maintain a Hardware Configuration Chart. The Hardware Configuration Chart is a graphic display of all hardware components that comprise a particular computer system or network of computer systems (multiple central processors linked together).

There are several significant advantages to having a documented hardware configuration. It:

1. Provides an illustrative vehicle for orienting and training new employees and for keeping present employees abreast of the most recent acquisitions
2. Aids in the hardware selection process
3. Aids programmers and systems analysts in the design process

Hardware configurations should be comprehensive showing all device entities that are interconnected via data lines. Off-line devices such as data reduction and electronic accounting machine devices are listed separately but not included in the graphic display of the hardware configuration.

Documentation Instructions

HARDWARE CONFIGURATION CHART—IV10

Instructions

Form: General Purpose, G10. The Hardware Configuration Chart may require a surface area longer than Form G10 can provide. In this case, a sheet of construction paper or poster board of sufficient size should be used.

Responsibility: Operations Manager.

Content: The Hardware Configuration Chart should graphically display the interrelationship (by data link) between all hardware components of a given computer system or network of computer systems.

1. List manufacturer, model number, and, if needed, device name on all devices. Use abbreviations.
2. List relevant speeds and/or capacities for devices (including communications lines) when appropriate.
3. Device symbols.

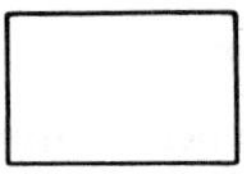

CPU, programmable communications controller, and primary storage.

Device controllers, modems, CPU and peripheral switches, and multiplexors.

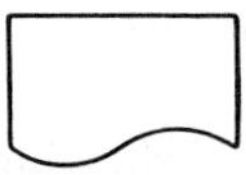

Printer (hardcopy output device).

Card reader (for card reader/punch include "CR/P" in interior of symbol; for punch only use simply "P").

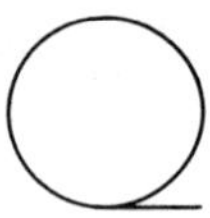

Magnetic tape.

Magnetic disk.

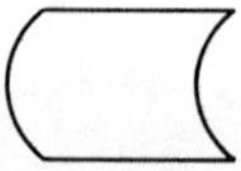

Mass storage (random access storage other than magnetic disk).

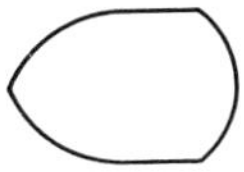

CRT. Include "CON" in interior of symbol for console.

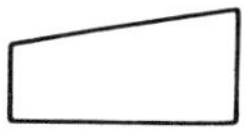

Hardcopy terminal. Include "CON" in interior of symbol for console.

Data link (local).

Communications link.

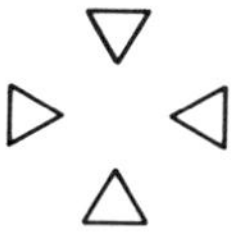

Data flow direction indicators.

4. Size of display. Use a single sheet of paper (or poster board) large enough to include all equipment for one computer system.
5. Level of detail. At least one Hardware Configuration Chart that includes all devices and their interrelationships should be prepared. Other charts that indicate only I/O devices or perhaps hardware applicable to a specific application area also may be prepared.
6. The hub of the Hardware Configuration Chart is the central processor(s) and the associated primary storage. Central processors that are not linked should be configured separately. The CPU is listed with its primary storage capacity (in bytes) in a rectangular box (e.g., IBM 370/158, 2 Meg). All devices should be connected directly, or indirectly via other devices, to the CPU.
7. Extended primary storage and primary storage shared with another computer should be illustrated separately from the CPU(s).
8. Magnetic disk. List capacity in millions of bytes. Note application area (or use) of dedicated disk drives (e.g., program library and operating system, payroll master file).
9. Magnetic tape. Note seven-track tapes with a "7" in the symbol. Note application area (or use) of dedicated tape devices.
10. Data flow lines. Use communication links to indicate linkage to remote locations. Use arrowheads to indicate direction of data flow to all devices.
11. Type of lines. Note whether communication lines are private, leased, dial-up, multidropped, etc. Note speed of lines in baud and whether simplex (SX), half duplex (HDX), or full duplex (FDX).
12. Note location of remote devices. Plant name, building name, room number, and/or city as applicable.

13. Colors. The judicious use of various colors results in a more usable configuration chart (e.g., green for 9600 baud lines, and yellow for 2400 baud lines).
14. Multiple similar terminal devices at remote locations. Instead of drawing 10 CRT symbols at a remote location, simply draw 1 and include the number "10" to indicate that there are 10 CRT's at that location.
15. Special features. On a separate General Purpose Form, G10, list, by devices, special features that might affect or limit the analysts or programmers in their design efforts (e.g., remote device cluster controller can handle up to 8 CRT's, but can be field upgraded to a maximum of 16).
16. Hardware scheduled to be replaced. Once a particular device has been scheduled to be deleted or replaced (and the replacement equipment has been ordered) place an asterisk "*" to the right of the device symbol and the date of deletion or replacement just under the asterisk on the configuration chart. Note the replacement device specifications under the special features for the old device.
17. Legends. Include a legend, if needed, to describe abbreviations that are seldom used or are peculiar to that chart only (e.g., DCC—Device Cluster Controller). CRT and IBM are examples of commonly used acronyms that should not be included in the legend.

9

Structural Organization and Personnel

Introduction

In order to formally establish personnel duties, lines of authority, and responsibilities, the computer center should be documented with a formal Organizational Chart, IV20, and a comprehensive set of Position Descriptions, IV30.

The Organizational Chart and Position Descriptions are imperative in an environment as dynamic as the computer center. Any changes in organization structure, committees, and/or personnel duties should be reflected on the Organizational Chart and/or the Position Descriptions, as applicable.

As a rule of thumb, the Data Processing Manager has the responsibility of updating the Organizational Chart and the Position Descriptions. However, this responsibility may reside with the Assistant DP Manager or someone in a commensurate staff position in larger computer centers.

Documentation Instructions

ORGANIZATIONAL CHART—IV20

Instructions

Form: General Purpose, G10. The Organizational Chart may require a surface area larger than Form G10 can provide. In this case, a sheet of construction paper or poster board of sufficient size should be used.

Responsibility: Data Processing Manager.

Content: The Organizational Chart graphically depicts the hierarchical organizational structure of the computer center.

1. Blocks. Use a rectangular box to denote each position (for exceptions, see number 8 below).
2. Position titles. Include the formal position title in the rectangular box.
3. Department title. Include the title of the department, division, office, etc., just above and to the left of the appropriate manager's box.
4. Positions of the same level. Place positions of the same organizational level horizontally adjacent to one another. For example, if the Systems, Programming, and Operations Managers are all considered to have roughly equivalent levels of responsibility, they should appear physically on the same level on the Organizational Chart. This does not apply to positions of different segments of the organization. For example, although systems analysts are usually considered at a higher level than operators, they could conceivably be at the same level on the chart since they are in different segments of the organization.
5. Line and staff. Each box denoting a position should be connected to at least one other box. These formal organizational lines (solid lines) indicate the formal lines of authority. All lines connecting line positions exit the bottom of the position box of the immediate superior. All lines connecting staff positions exit either side of the position box of the immediate superior.
6. Formal lines of communication outside the formal lines of authority. Often a manager of one department may wish to plan with another department manager, yet to do so according to the formal lines of communication would require involving the DP Manager. In many

cases this is unnecessary. Link those positions that have an ongoing need for formal communication outside of the lines of authority with a dotted line. Essentially these dotted lines document and approve certain often-used, informal, internal communications.

7. Positions of same level with no subordinates. In order to curtail excessive horizontal spreading of the chart, place boxes representing equal-level subordinates (who have no subordinates) vertically under their immediate superior.

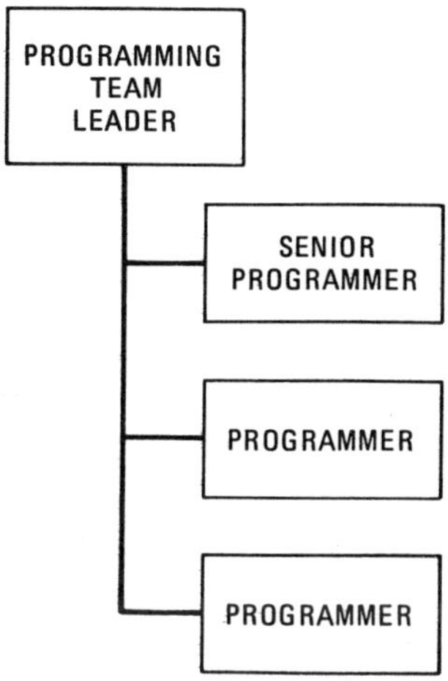

8. Group large numbers of similar positions into one box by including the position title (e.g., data entry operator) and the total number in that position in an insert in the upper right corner of the box.

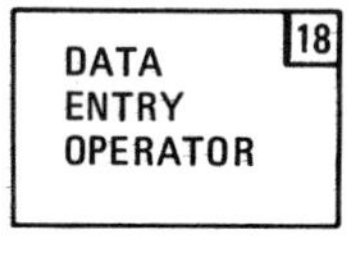

As a rule of thumb, note three or less in separate boxes and combine four or more in one box.

9. Standing committees. Place a symbol designation (asterisk, cross, etc.) by position titles that hold permanent positions on any internal or corporate standing committee or functional group (e.g., computer center steering committee, computer selection committee). Provide a symbol legend in the lower left corner of the Organizational Chart.

10. Multiple Organizational Charts. Very large computer centers may find having one Organizational Chart that includes only middle and upper level management and a set of detailed Organizational Charts for each separate department more helpful than one very large chart.

POSITION DESCRIPTION (PD)—IV30

Instructions

Form: General Purpose, G10.

Responsibility: Data Processing Manager.

Content: The Position Description provides instructions for documenting and describing all positions in the computer center. The various segments of the PD should be listed and discussed in the sequence of the instructions.

1. Position title. Assign a title (maximum of four words) that is roughly descriptive of the duties performed by the person holding that position.
2. Position code. A one- to four-character (alphanumeric) code designating a particular position (e.g., Apprentice Data Base Administrator—DBA2).
3. Function. This segment should discuss, in detail, the function to be performed. List and explain duties in as much detail as possible without limiting the flexibility required of the position. The duties discussions should be very specific at the lower levels and more general as the position responsibility increases.
4. Responsibility. Address major functional areas and position titles for which the person in that position is responsible. Be comprehensive.

Note: Certain "functions" may appear under "responsibilities" as well. If so, list in both places.

5. Interactions. List and discuss all formal and informal interactions that a person holding that position would have while performing the functions of that position. Do this by listing all titles of persons, both

internal and external to the company, who would interact with the person holding the named position. Also, discuss the fundamental reason for the interaction.

6. Standing committees. Name all standing committees, both internal and external to the computer center, of which the person holding the named position would be a member. When applicable, note the specific position on the committee (e.g., Chairman, nonvoting, etc.).

Note: List only those committees (or formal groups) for which the named position is a permanent or semipermanent (rotating) member. Do not list committees for which the person of the named position was elected or arbitrarily appointed.

7. Position requirements. List all minimum educational and experience prerequisites for the position. Also list any desirable education and experience that is over and above the minimum requirements. Label the former set of requirements "minimum" and the latter "desirable."
8. Salary level (optional). Use the standard corporate format for presenting salary data for a particular position.

Note: Since salary levels and ranges are constantly changing, some computer centers may opt to delete this segment in the PD's and keep this data readily available on a form that is more easily updated.

10

Training and Career Development

Introduction

The dynamic nature of the computer industry places demands on DP management to maintain an up-to-date and high level of expertise in the various career fields within DP. In order to do this effectively and efficiently, management should provide a comprehensive training program for every person in the computer center. The training program serves three major purposes:

1. To keep personnel at the state-of-the-art
2. To provide a training environment that is proactive rather than reactive
3. To provide a formal vehicle for career development

Training Program Implementation

The training program is established by DP management via a matching process that matches DP center objectives with the required training. Careful matching will also provide a career development plan for each position type. The effort required to prepare and maintain a comprehensive training program is considerable, but the expected dividends make the effort worthwhile. Significant increases in retention, internal upward mobility, morale, efficiency, and productivity become immediately apparent after the implementation of such a career development program.

The key to implementation of a training program is the DP Training Coordinator. The coordinator functions to:

1. Coordinate all DP training
2. Maintain training records on all DP personnel
3. Maintain files on available courses (content and accumulated critiques)

4. Plan and coordinate all in-house training programs
5. Select and provide training programs for in-house instructors
6. Schedule DP personnel in courses
7. Administer the DP training budget
8. Assist the immediate DP managers in the counseling of their personnel in career development

The Training Matrix

The Training Matrix, IV40, is the vehicle by which the entire training program is graphically displayed. Essentially the matrix indicates which courses are required, over time, for personnel in a particular position type.

Documentation Instructions and Forms

TRAINING MATRIX—IV40

Instructions

Form: The Training Matrix must be prepared individually for each company. The Form IV40, presented here, simply provides a model from which the matrix can be drawn. The size of the matrix would depend on the size of the company. The matrix can be completed on poster board or, more permanently, on metal (to be used with a grease pencil and/or magnets).

Responsibility: DP Training Coordinator.

Content: The Training Matrix is a graphical display of all required training for DP personnel. It is presented in a matrix format to facilitate the matching of courses, seminars, etc., with a particular position type. Also contained on the matrix are possible career paths for each position type.

The matrix is intended to show, for a particular position, the year by which a person should have completed the training specified.

> *Note:* The process of developing a Training Matrix is an iterative process that ultimately results in the best training program. The best approach is to conduct a series of DP management working sessions in order to establish training objectives. The Training Coordinator should meet individually with all managers to assist management in the process.

The working sessions decisions, both collective and individual, need to be made concerning:

- *a.* Position titles. If none exists, assign a title.
- *b.* Specialist positions. Identify various specialist types for all positions that have more than one person.
- *c.* Courses. Identify all general courses.
- *d.* Source of courses. Prioritize sources of courses (for each course) and estimate the required number of full-time equivalent days allotted to a particular course.
- *e.* Course/position match. Assign all courses that are desirable for a particular position. Indicate which are mandatory minimum requirements and which are recommended. Indicate the year by which the course should be completed.

f. Preparation of career path(s) for each position. Each position should have at least one advancement possibility. Two or more advancement possibilities should be noted only if appropriate.

1. Position types. Include the type of the position (usually the position title). Some DP position types that have more than one person are also listed as having specialist positions. Persons who are specialists within a position type may be given special training (all specialist positions are numbered on the right). The "general" position training applies to all persons with that title. Specialist training is over and above general training. For example, the "programmer" position will probably have specialists and would probably require at least four specialist positions for a medium-size computer center (e.g., scientific programmer, programming team leader, on-line systems, etc.). These would be listed as follows:

Programmer 1
Programmer 2
Programmer 3
Programmer 4
Programmer general

The numbered specialist positions would be defined on a separate General Purpose Form, G10.

2. Organizational brackets. The positions should be grouped according to the organizational structure. All organizational entities should be enclosed in brackets. Subbrackets (brackets within brackets) are appropriate when the organization has multiple levels. Label each bracket (e.g., programming section, data entry division, systems software, etc.). *Note:* Do not attempt to list the positions by salary level or rank.

3. Courses. The courses are listed across the top of the matrix. An attempt should be made to list these essentially by subject material even though there is overlap between certain areas (e.g., operations, data entry, programming, systems analysis, management, etc.).

The following is a partial listing of possible course areas applicable to most computer centers:

Fundamentals of computers and DP (one for in house personnel and one for user management)
Computer center orientation and applications
Use of the DP Documentation and Procedures Manual
Fundamentals of programming
Unit/record equipment and operation
Budget preparation and administration

Cost/benefit analysis
Techniques in conducting studies
Report preparation and presentation
Physical security
Facilities planning
Hardware/software evaluation and selection
Charting techniques and basic trend analysis
Keypunch operation
Key-to-disk (tape) operation
Basic supervisory training
Advanced supervisory training
OJT administration
Data entry management
Computer operations
Computer operations scheduling
Operations management
DP library management
Control of computer and information systems
Systems analysis and design
Advanced systems analysis and design
FORTRAN (basic)
FORTRAN (advanced)
COBOL (basic)
COBOL (advanced)
BAL (basic)
BAL (advanced)
Job control language (basic)
Job control language (advanced)
Advanced programming techniques
On-line systems design
Communications network design
Data base management systems
Operating systems (for a particular CPU series)
Distributed DP
Computer performance evaluation
Hardware/software failure and recovery (oriented to local specific applications)
Computer scheduling (internal priorities, etc.)

Simulation

Report writer and/or DBMS query languages

DP Documentation and Procedures Manual development and maintenance

DP project management

DP long-range planning

DP management

Advanced management

Privacy legislation

DP career development

Mini-micro computers

Process control

Each course should be briefly outlined to indicate the minimum requirements.

The number and scope of the courses will vary considerably among computer centers depending upon hardware and software used, type of industry, degree of specialization, and size of the computer center.

Also included in each course box would be coded letters that indicate the source of the course (the Training Coordinator would maintain a master file). The following are suggested codes:

I—Formal classes administered in-house by computer center personnel

D—DOD or Civil Service Commission courses (military and government only)

C—Commercially available

V—Vendor-supplied

X—Provided by consultants on a contract basis

N—College or university courses

P—Programmed instruction

OJT—On-the-job training

The sources are listed by code letter in the order in which the Training Coordinator will search for an offering of the course.

The number of full-time equivalent (8-hour) days the courses should be expected to take should be indicated in parentheses after the letter codes.

This illustration is an example of a typical course entry.

DP Long Range Planning C, X, V(3)

4. Legend of source-of-course letter codes. The letter codes for the source of the course should be listed here (see 3 above).
5. General legend area. This space is provided to list any local codes and their meaning.
6. Position types (user). Use the bottom lines of the matrix for the position types that are external to the computer center, but for which the computer center has a responsibility and/or an obligation to train (e.g., user management, operational users, etc.).
7. Position/course match. For a particular position type, place numbers in the boxes that correspond to the course required for that position. These numbers indicate three points:
   a. The course should be taken.
   b. The year, in that position, by which the course should be taken.

Note: A "2" does not necessarily mean that the course should be taken in the second year, but that it should be taken sometime within the first 2 years.

   c. Whether or not the course is mandatory or recommended (circled). Simply circle the number if the course is mandatory.

Note: The director of the computer center and all managers are assumed to have all appropriate training of their subordinates. Certain courses are noted for both subordinates and managers where the training is equally important to the managerial function and/or when timing is important.

8. Total number of training days, recommended or mandatory, for the first, second, and third (and later) years.

Note: Add the "general" training to the "specialist" training to get the total training program for a particular specialist position.

9. Total number of training days for a particular position (sum of 8 above).
10. Career path(s). The last two columns on the right side of the matrix indicate possible career path(s) for each position type. A career path is indicated progressively from left to right by the position type number (either side of matrix). To indicate two possible career paths divide each box by a slash (/). Position numbers above the slash indicate one path and those below indicate an alternative path. For those paths with multiple options for one path, use an "or" and

place all options within one box. To continue the career path progression, go to the highest level position type listed.

To illustrate, a senior programmer's career paths may be noted as:

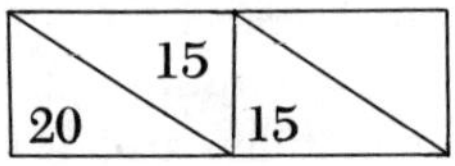

where: 15 is programming manager
20 is system software specialist.

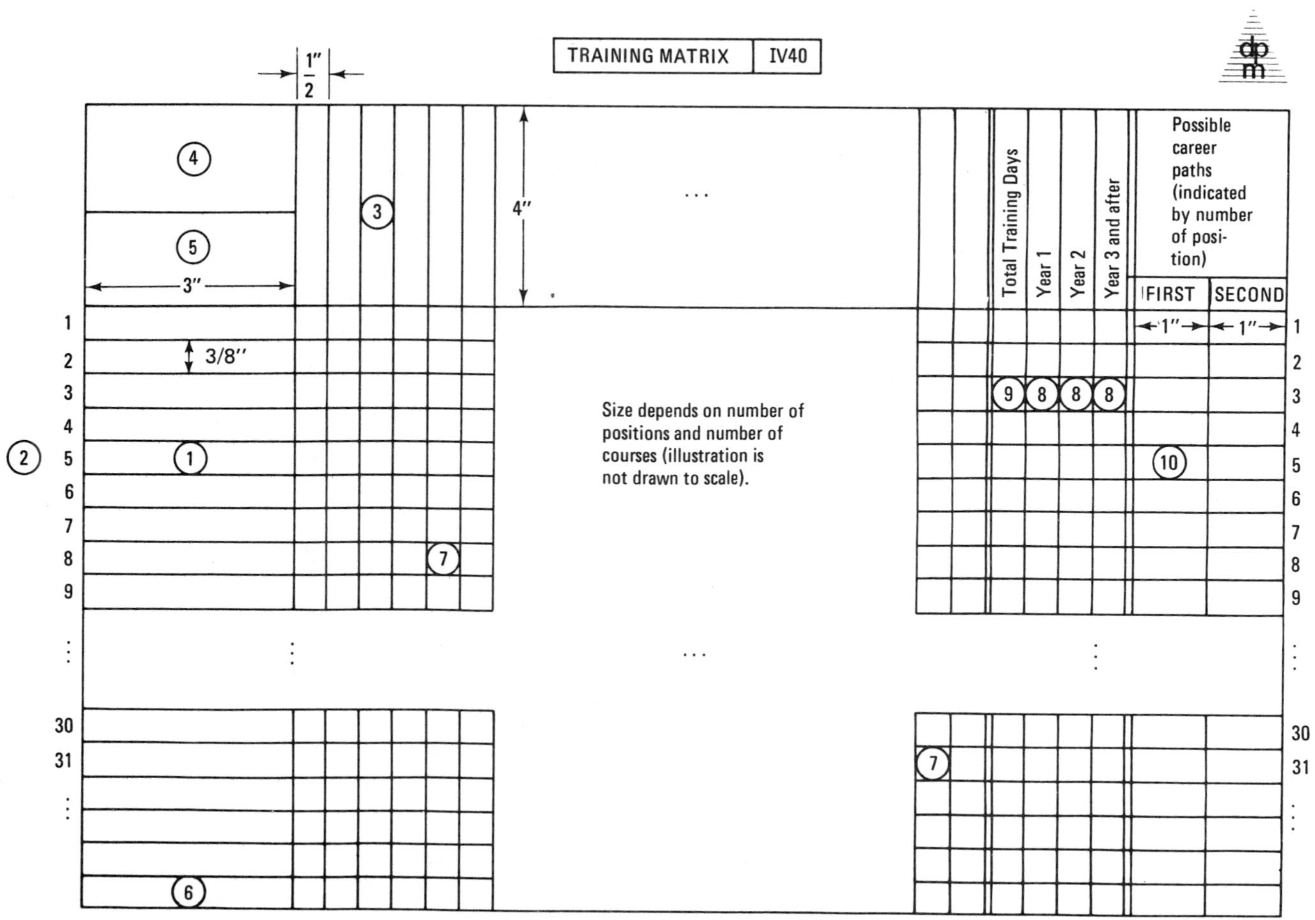
TRAINING MATRIX
IV40
1"/2
3"
4"
3/8"
1"
1"
Size depends on number of positions and number of courses (illustration is not drawn to scale).
Total Training Days
Year 1
Year 2
Year 3 and after
Possible career paths (indicated by number of position)
FIRST
SECOND
1
2
3
4
5
6
7
8
9
30
31
10

IV

Hardware and Software Evaluation and Selection

11

Hardware Evaluation and Selection

Introduction

The computer selection process can be executed in a variety of ways depending upon the expense and complexity of the equipment, the type of industry, and the level of sophistication of the computer center making the selection. This chapter contains a discussion of a step-by-step procedure that is intended to provide structure to the process via standardized forms and procedures. It is not intended to be all-encompassing but, instead, is intended to allow enough flexibility to accommodate the internal nuances of a given environment. For example, the forms were developed so the organization could include its own award criteria and the relative importance of each.

The interdependencies of hardware and software selection and evaluation dictate that the selection of one implies that due consideration was given to the effect of that selection on the other.

The Hardware Selection Committee

In order to obtain different perspectives about the various pieces of equipment and/or configurations, an ad hoc Hardware Selection Committee should be formed. The committee chairman should be from within the computer center. Other personnel should be selected from within the computer center and from among interested users.

Minor hardware acquisitions are those that do not significantly affect operations or procedures (i.e., memory upgrade, higher speed tape drives), and they should be accomplished without the formation of a committee.

Request for Information

The Request for Information (RFI) is optional in the selection process. The RFI serves two major purposes. It advises the buyer as to the scope and availability of hardware for the function in question, and it serves to more closely identify those vendors who have an interest in obtaining the organization's business.

The RFI is, as the name implies, a request for any available information regarding what equipment the vendor has that will address the problem briefly described in the RFI. The RFI is not meant to be a Request for Proposal (RFP). The contents of the RFI are detailed in the RFI instructions, V10.

Request for Proposal

The Request for Proposal (RFP) is a comprehensive document distributed to vendors requesting that they, should they so desire, propose a hardware configuration to meet the company's data processing needs. The RFP contains the following forms:

V20—RFP (text material)
V30—Hardware/Software Vendor Questionnaire
V40—System Characteristics
V50—Cost Summary
V60—Benchmark Results

The RFP basically has two parts. The first part, or the text of the RFP, V20, is descriptive and illustrative with respect to the current computer environment and the computer center's needs. The second part consists of a set of questions to be addressed by the vendor and two (three if a benchmark is required) other forms to be completed by the vendor. It is important that the vendors use the standardized formats of Forms V40, V50, and V60, so that evaluation of the relative strengths and weaknesses of the various vendors is not disguised by each vendor by using a different approach to present his or her equipment.

It is recommended that the RFP's be distributed in a joint meeting of the computer center personnel, users (if part of a selection committee), and vendors. In this meeting the RFP can be explained in detail and vendors can ask any questions necessary to clarify any parts of the RFP that are not clear. The joint meeting eliminates the possibility of unknowingly giving an unfair advantage to a vendor.

User Surveys As an Aid to Evaluation

The User Survey, V70, is a Request for Information about the proposed hardware from computer centers that have the proposed hardware installed.

The survey can be used to amplify and/or verify information contained in the RFP response.

Evaluation of Responses to the RFP

The responses to the RFP should be evaluated by the hardware selection committee (if one exists) based on the award criteria set forth in the RFP. The Proposal Evaluation Worksheet, V80, can be used by the individual committee members for giving relative point values and rankings for each criterion and for using cumulative totals to aid in the selection of a vendor. The worksheet can also be used to summarize the various individual points and rankings.

Standardized Forms

The standardized instructions and forms that follow are equally applicable to hardware and software evaluation and selection. The examples are given for hardware only unless a software example is also needed, in which case both are given.

Documentation Instructions and Forms

REQUEST FOR INFORMATION (RFI)—V10

Instructions

Form: Letterhead.

Responsibility: Data Processing Manager.

Content: The Request for Information (RFI) is a cover letter that presents general information on the present computer environment and the type of computer hardware/software needed. It is sent at the discretion of the DPM to appropriate suppliers. The purposes of the RFI are to canvass the marketplace and to determine which suppliers have viable alternatives and/or are willing to compete for the business.

Note: The RFI is recommended for all major hardware additions or replacements that would have a significant effect on the direction of the computer center, and for virtually all software acquisitions. However, the RFI should be omitted when alternatives are well known and understood by in-house personnel. In such a case, the Request for Proposal would be the next step.

1. RFI cover letter. Include the name, city, and state of all suppliers in the addressee portion. The letter should explain the purpose of the RFI. It should also limit the written response to three to five pages. There should be no limit placed on promotional material.
2. The text of the RFI should include:
   - *a.* Introduction. A general description of the computing environment and the changes in operations or technology that prompted the RFI. The make-up of the selection committee and a brief RFI content synopsis should be included.
   - *b.* Historical perspective. Functions and applications that have been, are, and/or will be supported by the computer center.
   - *c.* Present computer center configuration. Include a computer system configuration chart and explanations where applicable.
   - *d.* Statement of problem. A brief statement of the problem causing a requirement for additional and/or replacement hardware.
   - *e.* Constraints or limitations. A brief description of constraints or limitations that might tend to eliminate certain vendors (i.e., money, time, speeds, size, etc.).

REQUEST FOR PROPOSAL—V20

Instructions

Form: None.

Responsibility: Data Processing Manager.

Content: The text of the Request for Proposal (RFP) is that portion of the RFP that describes the environment, objectives, and the mechanics and criteria of the selection process. If an RFI was submitted, number 1 below can be omitted.

1. Introduction. A general description of the computing environment, past and present, as it relates to the hardware/software to be acquired. This would include application systems, present hardware configurations, and constraints or limitations. (See RFI, V10.)
2. Objectives. Detail all objectives that relate to the proposed hardware/software. If the objectives are time phased, present them by year. This section should be comprehensive so the vendor has an accurate picture of the needs of the organization. For example, for hardware acquisitions, to maximize packaged software availability, to reduce response time while reducing per-unit time charges, to have a compatible COBOL compiler, to provide for continued compatible growth, etc.
3. Approach. Describe all alternative approaches that are being considered within the computer center.
4. Guidelines for the RFP responses (proposals).
   a. Scope of the proposal (multiple proposals, combined proposals from more than one manufacturer, etc.).
   b. Format of proposal. Part one should be a management summary that does not exceed 5 to 10 single-spaced typewritten pages depending upon the complexity of the proposed configuration or proposed software. (The required forms are not considered part of the 5 to 10 pages.) The vendor is free to format the contents of the management summary as he wishes. To maintain uniformity the use of binders should be rejected or requested. Part two is any additional material required to support the management summary (i.e., user manuals, applications descriptions, pictures, etc.). The number of copies of part

one should be specified. Only one copy of part two need be submitted except under unusual circumstances.

c. Response deadline. Date by which a response to the RFP must be submitted in order to be placed in consideration.

5. Presentation of costs. The manner in which the costs are to be presented should be specified. For example, prices can be purchase only, lease, lease/purchase, etc. If vendors are asked to present prices over several years, a common format should be followed by all respondents. If discounted costs are used, then the discount rate, tax rate, and depreciation schedules should be included. The explanation for completion of the Cost Summary, V50, should be included in this section.
6. References. The vendor should be asked to supply the names, addresses, and telephone numbers of organizations that use the proposed hardware/software in a similar environment. The vendor should be responsible for the initial contact.
7. Award procedure. The date by which selections will be made should be included. Describe who will make the decision and on what basis (i.e., weighted point system, vote of committee, etc.).
8. Award criteria. Describe each award criterion and its relative importance by assigning each a point value from 5 to 95. The total number of points should equal 100. The award criteria and their relative importance are, of course, arbitrary; however, the following criteria are suggested as options for hardware selection.

   a. Total system cost. Includes costs for equipment, software, maintenance, and extraordinary personnel support.

   b. Availability of software. Availability is defined as quality, quantity, and cost (not included in "a" above). Applications and system software may be considered as one criterion or considered separately as two criteria.

   c. System flexibility. Refers to the ability to accommodate changes in capacity or nature of activity with few, if any, significant system (hardware or software) changes.

   d. System reliability and overall quality of the vendor. This criterion includes considerations for total system availability, system mean time between failures, equipment mean and maximum time to repair, and procedures for system restart. The overall quality of the vendor is self-explanatory. Under certain circumstances, system reliability and overall quality of the vendor may be considered separately as two criteria.

e. Compatibility with existing activities. This criterion reflects on the effort required to integrate the new capabilities into the existing environment.

f. Backup. This criterion is primarily used when considering main frames. It reflects the willingness of users of the similar systems to act as backup sites and the distance to these sites.

g. Overall evaluation. This criterion allows for giving credit for items not included in other criteria as well as for interrelationships between categories that make the total more or less than the sum of the parts.

The following award criteria are suggested as options for software selection.

a. Total system cost. Included should be costs of software, any modifications, maintenance, and extraordinary personnel support.

b. System flexibility. Refers to the ability to accommodate changes in capacity or nature of activity with few, if any, significant system (hardware or software) changes.

c. System reliability and overall quality of the vendor. This criterion refers to the performance record of a particular software package. A new package unproven in a user environment should rate very low. The overall quality of the vendor is self-explanatory. Under certain circumstances, system reliability and overall quality of the vendor may be considered separately as two criteria.

d. Compatibility with existing activities. This criterion reflects on the effort required to integrate the proposed software with existing, functionally adjacent software and/or application areas. *Note:* If required modifications are to be accomplished by the vendor then less weight should be given to this criterion since the modifications will then be included in the total system cost. (See item "a.")

e. Compatibility with existing hardware. Refers to the capability of the present hardware configurations to accommodate the new software. *Note:* As is often the case, a planned commensurate upgrade in hardware capabilities would tend to place less emphasis on this criterion.

f. Input/output. Reflects on how well the system I/O meets the company's needs.

g. Efficiency. This criterion refers to the ability of the software package to accomplish the stated objectives while minimizing the use of resources, mainly personnel and hardware.

h. Overall evaluation. This criterion allows for giving credit for items not included in other criteria as well as for interrelationships between categories that make the total more or less than the sum of the parts.

9. Implementation schedule. Most likely and/or optimistic and pessimistic implementation dates should be included. An explanation is appropriate if the elapsed time between vendor selection and installation/implementation is extraordinarily short or long.

10. New system requirements. This section enumerates the basic requirements that are expected to be met by any proposed system. This section is difficult to generalize; therefore, the following are only examples of topics (hardware only) that might be addressed. It is likely that this section may require a time-phased presentation (i.e., 600-lpm printer upgraded to a 1000-lpm printer in 18 months.

    a. Hardware requirements (printer, disk, number of ports, speeds, capacities, quality, etc.)

    b. Software packages (applications and systems)

    c. Maximum on-line response times at various user loads

    d. Compilers and interpreters required

11. Contact persons. Vendors should be restricted in the persons with whom they are allowed to make contact. The names, departments, titles, and telephone numbers of approved contact persons should be listed.

HARDWARE/SOFTWARE VENDOR QUESTIONNAIRE—V30

Instructions

Form: None.

Responsibility: Chairman, selection committee (for compilation of questions); vendor representative (for responding to questions).

Content: Under normal circumstances many questions will surface that should be addressed by responding vendors in order that the proposed systems can be adequately evaluated. The questions should be contained in an appendix to the RFP. The generalization of these questions is difficult; however, the following are presented as example questions and/or points that could be addressed depending on the scope of the proposed hardware acquisition. The list is merely an example and is not intended to be exhaustive. The questions are in an outline format so that the vendors' responses will be similarly formatted. Since the responses to these questions are an appendix to the management summary, the responses are not part of the 5- to 10-page management summary.

The wide variety of commercially available proprietary software precludes the generalization of a vendor questionnaire; therefore, the example questionnaire shown below is illustrative of a questionnaire for hardware selection only. The general format would be the same for software selection.

I. SOFTWARE (relative to the hardware acquisition)

A. Operating System

1. Job control language (JCL)

a. JCL differences between batch and interactive environments.

b. Prompting when the interactive user makes a JCL error.

c. Abbreviation of JCL commands.

2. Resource allocation

a. Memory.

b. Disk. Does disk space have to be preallocated?

c. Peripheral equipment. Is input and output spooled?

3. Software recovery

a. Levels of recovery after a system hang. Are executing jobs restarted from the beginning, at point of interruption, etc.?

- *b.* Fail soft capability when part of the hardware goes down. Is it automatic or under operator control?
- *c.* Are timesharing/on-line sessions restarted at point of interruption?
- *d.* Power failure features.

4. Logging, accounting, and verification
   - *a.* Accounting for resources used (e.g., CPU time, disk, print output, etc.).
   - *b.* Control of the amount of resources available to a user.
   - *c.* Control of privileges given the user.
5. Operator requirements
   - *a.* To run timesharing/on-line only.
   - *b.* To run timesharing/on-line and batch.
   - *c.* Scheduling done by the operator.
   - *d.* Status information available to the operator.
6. System scheduler
   - *a.* Priority determination.
     - *1)* Timesharing/on-line
     - *2)* Batch
   - *b.* User supplied priority (can the user ask for a higher priority?).
   - *c.* Operator override/control.
7. Multiprogramming capability
   - *a.* Number of simultaneously running batch/timesharing/on-line jobs (theoretical and practical limits).
   - *b.* Memory management and protection (hardware features to facilitate same).
   - *c.* Limit on job or task memory size.
   - *d.* Hardware to lower overhead.
8. Ease of use
   - *a.* "Help" commands.
   - *b.* Sign-on procedures (automatic procedures at log-on or job initiation).
   - *c.* Catalog procedures for files and programs.
   - *d.* Log-on messages.
   - *e.* News files.
   - *f.* Mail box facility.
   - *g.* Provision for on-line consulting.

B. Programming Languages (compiler/interpreter)—Standards met, extensions to standards, standard features not implemented, nonstandard areas, anticipated upgrades to existing language, debugging tools and aids

1. Procedure-oriented languages

2. Problem-oriented languages

3. I/O system language interfaces, restrictions, special requirements, extensions, device independency

C. Other Software

1. Computer assisted instruction (CAI)

2. Statistical packages

a. Types of files used.

b. Interactive/batch/both.

3. Library of contributed software from other users

4. Text editor for programming

5. Text and document processing system

6. Software support for on-line documentation

7. Data Base Management Systems

a. Manufacturer supplied.

b. Commercially available compatible DBMS's.

c. Memory overload required to run.

8. Mass storage access methods

a. Types.

b. Languages interfaced (calls or part of the language).

9. Scope of utility programs

10. Language translators

a. Type of conversion.

b. Percent efficiency.

11. Emulator and/or simulators available

II. COMMUNICATIONS CAPABILITIES

A. ASCII terminal support

B. Synchronous terminal support

C. RJE support protocols

D. Front end computer support available

E. Remote concentrator support available

F. Expansion capabilities

G. Speeds available

H. Types of computer networks supported

I. Automatic log-off for inactive terminals

III. HARDWARE

A. Central Processing Unit

1. Processor speed (benchmark)

2. Instruction set (types of instructions, number)

3. Registers (number, types, speeds)

4. Multiprocessing capabilities

B. Memory

1. Type (manufacturing technique, word size, cache, extended)

2. Capacity (proposed and maximum)

3. Address ability (at bit, byte (size), and word level)

4. Cycle time

5. Virtual memory (hardware features in support of it)

6. Parity (detection, correction)

C. Mass Storage (disks)

1. Capacity (per drive, total)

2. Access time (maximum, minimum, average)

3. Transfer rate

4. Packs fixed or interchangeable

5. Control unit required

D. Tape Drive

1. Number of tracks

2. Density

3. Speed over R/W head

4. Access

5. Auto load/unload

6. Control unit required

E. Card Reader

1. Speed

2. Code(s) accepted

F. Printer

1. Type (chain, matrix, character, line, etc.)

2. Character set (interchangeable)

3. Speed (cps or lpm)

- *G.* Card Punch
  - *1.* Speed
  - *2.* Code(s)
- *H.* I/O Channels
  - *1.* Types/numbers
  - *2.* Transfer rate

IV. ENVIRONMENT/POWER REQUIREMENTS

- *A.* Power (electrical) requirements
  - *1.* Voltage
  - *2.* Amps
  - *3.* Cycles
  - *4.* Wires, phases
  - *5.* High, low limits (also, does machine protect itself?)
- *B.* Environmental
  - *1.* Ambient air temperture, humidity ranges
  - *2.* Air-conditioning heat load
  - *3.* Special requirements such as chilled water, etc.

V. ACCESS CONTROLS

- *A.* Features to control access to the computing system (e.g., user accounts, authorizations, etc.)
  - *1.* Hardware
  - *2.* Software
- *B.* Protection of operating system programs and files

VI. MISCELLANEOUS

- *A.* Expandability (increments, cost, field upgrade?)
  - *1.* CPU
  - *2.* Memory
  - *3.* Ports
  - *4.* Disk
  - *5.* Tape
  - *6.* Unit record I/O units
  - *7.* Channels
- *B.* Reliability (mean time before failure and mean time to recovery)
  - *1.* Software
  - *2.* Hardware

C. Maintenance Support
  1. Software
  2. Hardware
D. Personnel services (availability and costs)
  1. Installation
  2. Maintenance
  3. Training

SYSTEM CHARACTERISTICS—V40

Instructions

Form: V40.

Responsibility: Chairman, selection committee (for definition of system characteristics); vendor representative (for completion).

Content: The System Characteristics form allows the organization an opportunity to list features that are of particular interest to them. It is not a specifications sheet; but it is intended to display cost, availability, and comments regarding these features.

1. Features. The organization should simply list by category (preferably in outline format) those features for which it would like to have more detailed cost and availability information. In hardware selection, for example, an abbreviated list might be as follows:
   a. Support software
   b. Mass storage access methods
   c. Data base management systems
   d. Utility programs

   In software selection an abbreviated list might be:
   a. Personnel training
      1) Programmers
      2) Users

   b. Compatibility under
      1) DOS
      2) OS
2. Included in bid. If the feature is included, the vendor should place a "yes" by feature and reference the item of cost under which it is included. For example, utilities programs might be included under the operating system cost.
3. Availability. The vendor should include the feature's expected date of availability and its cost, if known. An approximate cost may be entered but should be so labeled.
4. Comments. This space is provided for the vendor to make clarifying comments, if necessary.
5. Total number of Form V40 pages.
6. Page number.

REPORT TITLE SYSTEM CHARACTERISTICS	NO. V40	DATE	VENDOR

FEATURE	Included in Bid	Available		Comments
		Date	Cost	
(1)	(2)	(3)		(4)

COST SUMMARY—V50

Instructions

Form: V50.

Responsibility: Vendor representative.

Content: The Cost Summary provides a vehicle by which costs can be presented in a standard format for ease of comparison among vendors. The costs can be presented over time if future system upgrades are proposed.

There are several approaches to completion of a time-phased Cost Summary. The organization should specify the desired approach in the text of the RFP. For purchased hardware/software the approaches could be as follows:

A. Costs are not discounted. The totals reflect the absolute cost for each of the respective years.

B. Costs are discounted at a rate given in the text of the RFP before consideration of taxes and depreciation.

C. Costs are discounted after consideration of taxes and depreciation. Tax rates and depreciation schedules should be included in the text of the RFP. For leasing, the best approach would be to include rental cost to reflect the absolute cost for the respective years. The "total" column is not used when costs are rental figures.

A responding vendor may wish to present cost figures on the Cost Summary for purchase, lease, and/or lease/purchase.

1. Item. The organization should list the categories and items for which it desires a cost breakdown. For example (not meant to be comprehensive):
   a. Equipment
      1) Main frame
      2) Disk subsystem
      3) Tape subsystem
      4) Communications
      5) Peripherals (specify)
   b. Software
      1) Operating system
      2) Compilers (specify)
      3) Major packages (specify)

c. Maintenance Costs
  1) Plan A (specify)
  2) Plan B (specify)

d. Other Costs (specify)

e. Discounts

2. Initial purchase/rent. The initial outlay at installation time or monthly rental and the description and/or number of the unit (e.g., 301 Mass storage unit, $26,000). Strike out purchase or rent in the column heading, as appropriate.
3. Years 2, 3, 4, and 5. Any subsequent upgrades are included in the appropriate year in the format of number 2 above.
4. Total. For purchased prices only.
5. Total net cost. The costs of each year are totaled and presented for each maintenance plan proposed.
6. Total number of V50 pages.
7. Page number.

REPORT TITLE	COST SUMMARY	NO. V50	DATE	VENDOR

ITEM	Init. Purc./Rent		Year 2		Year 3		Year 4		Year 5		Total	
	Desc.	Cost	Desc.	Cost	Desc.	Cost	Desc.	Cost	Desc.	Cost	Desc.	Cost
(1)	(2)		(3)								(4)	
Total Net Cost, with:	(5)											

Page (7)/(6)

BENCHMARK RESULTS—V60

Instructions

Form: V60.

Responsibility: Chairman, selection committee (for definition of benchmarks); vendor representative (for completion).

Content: The Benchmark Results form provides the vendor with a vehicle for presenting the benchmark results. A form of this type is intended for only the most basic type of information. The form is appropriate for both hardware and software benchmarks.

1. Job name. Include the name of the job and/or jobs executed.
2. Circumstances. If circumstances are to be varied (e.g., memory size, number of terminals on-line, etc.), include a description of the appropriate circumstances.
3. CPU time. CPU time used during compilations and/or execution of the job. Time should be in seconds.
4. Elapsed time. The total elapsed time (wall clock) from job initiation until end-of-job. Time should be in minutes.
5. Response time. The average total elapsed time from just after a remote user makes an inquiry until a response is received.
6. Miscellaneous. This column is for any other arbitrary criteria that the organization feels would aid in evaluating the benchmark results. Leave blank if not required.
7. Comments. This space is provided so that the vendor can add comments if the benchmark run was executed under other than the prescribed environment.
8. Number of V60 pages.
9. Page number.

USER SURVEY—V70

Instructions

etterhead.

oility: Chairman, selection committee.

The User Survey is a vehicle by which proposal material can be and/or verified by existing users of the proposed hardware/ The selection committee chairman should write and/or call users gested by the vendor or known to the chairman for the purpose of information.

uestions posed to these users should be directly or indirectly the established award criteria. For example, a possible inquiry any available mean-time-between-failure statistics to support any ims as to system reliability (for hardware).

REPORT TITLE BENCHMARK RESULTS	NO. V60	DATE	VENDOR

Job Name	Circumstances	CPU Time (seconds)	Elapsed Time (minutes)	Response Time (seconds)	(6)	Comments
(1)	(2)	(3)	(4)	(5)		(7)

REPORT TITLE BENCHMARK RESULTS	NO. V60	DATE	VENDOR

Job Name	Circumstances	CPU Time (seconds)	Elapsed Time (minutes)	Response Time (seconds)	(6)	Comments
(1)	(2)	(3)	(4)	(5)		(7)

Page (9)/(8)

USER SURVEY—V70

Instructions

Form: Letterhead.

Responsibility: Chairman, selection committee.

Content: The User Survey is a vehicle by which proposal material can be amplified and/or verified by existing users of the proposed hardware/software. The selection committee chairman should write and/or call users either suggested by the vendor or known to the chairman for the purpose of gathering information.

The questions posed to these users should be directly or indirectly related to the established award criteria. For example, a possible inquiry may be for any available mean-time-between-failure statistics to support any vendor claims as to system reliability (for hardware).

PROPOSAL EVALUATION WORKSHEET—V80

Instructions

Form: V80.

Responsibility: Chairman, selection committee.

Content: The Proposal Evaluation Worksheet is used to graphically display both individual and cumulative evaluations of each proposal. The matrix format allows for presentation of points (out of 100) relative to the other criteria and ranking relative to the other vendors with respect to a given criterion. The total points given each proposal are accumulated for the "bottom line."

1. Vendor. The names of the vendors submitting proposals (e.g., IBM, CDC, DEC, etc.).
2. Criterion. Each criterion with its associated relative point value would be placed in the respective boxes [e.g., system flexibility (15 points), system reliability/support (10 points), etc]. See the RFP instructions, V20 (item 8), for suggested criteria.
3. Points/criterion. An evaluator places the points out of the total number allotted that he/she feels are merited (e.g., 10 of 15 for system flexibility).
4. Rank. Numerical rank of each proposal based on the number of points given a particular criterion.
5. Total number of points. Accumulation of all points for one proposal.
6. Overall rank. Ranking based on the total number of points.

Note: Committee member evaluations are compiled on separate V80's and then summarized on a separate V80 worksheet form.

REPORT TITLE	PROPOSAL EVALUATION WORKSHEET	NO. V80	DATE

	①							
②	③ ④							
TOTAL POINTS OVERALL RANK	⑤ ⑥							

12

Software Evaluation and Selection

Introduction

The procedures set forth for hardware selection and evaluation in Chapter 11 are also applicable to software selection and evaluation. Therefore, frequent explicit and/or implied references will be made to the material presented in Chapter 11. This procedure enables the Software Selection Committee (established in a similar manner as the Hardware Selection Committee) enough flexibility to accommodate the internal nuances of a given environment.

The basic difference between hardware and software selection is the number of options available to the potential buyer. It is not unreasonable to expect that a buyer of hardware may have fewer than 10 viable options from which to choose, whereas, on the other hand, the potential buyer of software may have a cumbersome number of options, for example, 50. Perhaps the initial screening of software options is the most difficult step in the software selection and evaluation process.

The interdependencies of hardware and software selection and evaluation dictate that the selection of one implies that due consideration was given to the effect of that selection on the other.

Categories of Commercially Available Proprietary Software

Proprietary (or packaged) software can be placed logically into three basic categories with each having several subcategories. These categories are systems software, applications software, and systems development and management software.

1. Systems software
   a. Data storage, retrieval, and manipulation (DBMS's, query languages, utilities, etc.)

   - *b.* Software management (software resource accounting and optimization)
   - *c.* Hardware management (hardware resource accounting and optimization)
2. Applications software
   - *a.* By application area (payroll, accounts receivable, inventory, etc.)
   - *b.* By industry type (manufacturing, local government, universities, banking, etc.)
3. Systems development and management software
   - *a.* Debugging aids
   - *b.* Documentation aids
   - *c.* Programming language conversion aids
   - *d.* DP project management aids

Sources of Information for Software Selection

Several publishers compile data on proprietary software. International Computer Programs, Inc., Datapro Research Corporation, and the Technical Publishing Company (Datamation) are among the most visible. ICP offers a semiannual series detailing the specifications of the available software packages. Datapro offers a continuously updated series with specifications and evaluations. In cooperation with Datapro, Datamation publishes annually a summary of user ratings of the more popular software products.

A first step in the software selection process would be to examine publications, such as those mentioned above, in order to identify vendors that offer the desired product.

The Request for Information

The RFI is usually a requirement in most software decision processes because of the necessity to screen some vendors in order to achieve a manageable list of options. The fundamental purposes of the RFI are the same for both hardware and software selection.

Request for Proposal

The RFP is a comprehensive document distributed to vendors requesting that they, should they so desire, propose software—either available, to be developed, and/or modified—as appropriate, to meet the company's data processing needs. The RFI-RFP format (Forms V10, V20, V30, V40, V50, and V60) as discussed in Chapter 11 is equally applicable to software selection.

User Surveys as an Aid to Evaluation

The User Survey, V70, as in hardware selection, is appropriate for software selection.

Evaluation of Responses to the RFP

The Proposal Evaluation Worksheet, V80, as in hardware selection, is appropriate for software selection.

Appendix

Abbreviations Used in the DP Manual

AD	Applications Description, I10
BA	batch processing
CC	computer center
DBMS	Data Base Management System
Doc.	documentation or document
DP	data processing
DPM	Data Processing Manager
DP Manual	Data Processing Documentation and Procedures Manual
FC	Flowchart
FS	feasibility study
FST	feasibility study team
FSTH	feasibility study team head
GP	General Purpose form, G10
ISPC	Information Systems Policy Committee
ISPCH	Information Systems Policy Committee Head
LP	lead programmer
OL	on-line
OM	Operations Manager
PD	Position Description
PT	project team
PTH	project team head
RC	review coordinator
REV	revised
SA	systems analyst
SC	systems coordinator

SSR	System Status Report, I140
SYS	system
UH	user head(s)—refers collectively to all heads of departments, divisions and/or agencies involved in the development and operation of a given system

Index